COUNTING CHICKENS

For a complete list of Management Books 2000 titles,
visit our web-site on http://www.mb2000.com

COUNTING CHICKENS
The 'Nexus' Principles for Personal and Professional Development

Phil Olley

2000

To Mum – for your final words
To Elizabeth – for ALL your words and deeds
To Christopher & Victoria – for all the Fun

First published in 2003 by Management Books 2000 Ltd
Forge House, Limes Road
Kemble, Cirencester
Gloucestershire, GL7 6AD, UK
Tel: 0044 (0) 1285 771441/2
Fax: 0044 (0) 1285 771055
E-mail: m.b.2000@virgin.net
Web: mb2000.com

Printed and bound in Great Britain by Biddles, Guildford

British Library Cataloguing in Publication Data is available
ISBN 1-85252-425-1

Acknowledgements

To Glen McCoy, for making me do it, and for significant injections of inspiration, direction, and material.

To all those who have done similar before - all the management, personal development and business writers and speakers who I read and listen to avidly.

To all those I've coached, individually or in groups - I learn from you as well.

To the writers of Great Books, the makers of Great Films, the players of Great Music, and the doers of Great Deeds whose inspiration surrounds me daily and who create the legacy for us all.

To my editor and publisher, James Alexander, at Management Books, for his good work in producing this book from my texts and diagrams.

Contents

Contents

Section One

'Counting Chickens'

1

What's It All About?

Before I answer the age-old chicken and egg question, let me just put this book into context.

This is not a book about 'All you ever needed to know about running a business but were afraid to ask' – the twenty-four hour solution to any business.

Nor is it a book about chickens as the first section might imply (at least, not in the strict sense, but more of that later). So, if you have found it on the reading list for Agricultural publications, take it from me – it's probably not what you want.

- **If you run a small business**, on the other hand (either a small trader, or a family business, or a professional practice), and you sometimes can't see the wood for the trees (or the chickens for the feathers), or if you are considering taking that first step into business, then it is definitely for you.

- **But it's not a book purely for beginners.** Many of the businesses you and I encounter on a daily basis (so-called 'established' companies) would do well to re-establish these principles.

- **And ... it's not purely a book about running a business.** This book is designed to help anyone who needs to stay on top of their game, to remain at their most effective and at peak performance on the business battleground.

- **It is for you if you are an executive or professional** who needs to be effective in order to not simply survive in the modern business world, but who wants to reach forward to your next mountain or move up again on the career ladder.

- **It is for anyone who seeks to improve performance enhance results, and get more from any aspect of life ... whether it's business growth, personal happiness or financial success.**

- **It is for you if you want to 'self coach'** using personal development tools which are practical, tried and tested and proven.

- **It is for you if you are a manager, supervisor, sales team leader, or in-house coach, mentor or line manager** ... in short if you have any responsibility for the professional development of others.

- **It is for you if you are a business coach, personal development trainer, or the more-enlightened type of business consultant** who believes in the result over the text-book model.

And whether you are running a business or you are employed, it is your entrepreneurial talents which will set you apart in the 21st century. I have used the setting up and running of a business as a theme representing a goal. But the concepts, levers, tools and stratagrams can be applied equally well to any professional or personal goal. Indeed those who succeed in the modern world will be those who are most able to view themselves as the CEO of their life, and all its facets.

It is interesting to note that most people who work in employed positions, when asked what their ideal life would consist of, include the goal of setting up their own business – whether it be as a consultant in their current field, or by switching to a particular passion or hobby, setting up a coffee shop, and so on.

If you want the musings and theories of a Harvard graduate ... again this book is not for you.

My own observation is that most of the serious breakthroughs in the modern business world, from the most effective executives in organisations or from sole entrepreneurs, are non-Harvard, non-MBA in nature. Indeed, I have met many graduates from these schools who (whilst excellent business consultants or professionals in their own right), by their own admittance wouldn't have a clue how to handle the slings and arrows of setting up and developing a business from scratch, nor would they have the desire to do so. And most business breakthroughs are created by people who have 'failed', even been bankrupt, and learned how to do it another way – who have created their own success. This is where we can find not a Business Model, but a toolkit of tactics and strategies and techniques which can be employed, often as 'second-nature', to achieve massive business results. This is where we find the guerrilla tactics, the simplest and most effective tools, which will allow you to get ahead and which, if we can deliver them to others, can similarly help them to turn their own dreams into realities.

This is a book by a person such as you. Not by someone steeped in management-speak, or who has spent years at business school. What you will get from this book is a set of principles to guide you in your day-to-day activities, and help to turn your vision, your dream, into reality. **And, after all, turning dreams into reality is what business is all about – isn't it –? It's about pursuing a vision and making it happen.**

The first challenge is to open the book, open your mind, and be prepared to follow through from start to finish.

Mother told me there would be lifetimes like this!

'Don't count your chickens before they hatch!'

It's a favourite enthusiasm squasher, isn't it? It isn't said with any malevolence, of course, but with a sage-like care for our feelings. That's why it's the people who care most for us who are more likely to offer it as advice.

And I'm sure I'm not alone – but my mother said it countless times. And never in connection with anything particularly important. Usually in connection with little things I looked forward to. It's a way of sheltering us in advance from potential disappointments. And now … like our parents before us, I find myself biting my lip when I'm about to say it to my children.

So a paradigm of disappointment avoidance is generated in all of us, by our parents' well-meaning words of wisdom, doubtless resulting from years of having the same passed to them by their parents. We inherit this model of the world – and ultimately it limits us.

But before you think we can blame it all on previous generations, think again. I'm not one to apportion blame. It's not about blame. But it's an explanation as to why such paradigms, such beliefs, such models of the way we think the world works are allowed to go unchallenged. The disappointment avoidance technique is a means of survival, of saving face, in the world at large.

'Don't count your chickens ...'

Ouch – someone's broken my model!

Many people are fortunate to have this limitation burst asunder by a searing insight, or an occurrence so outrageous that the foundation is rocked and causes them to dramatically rebuild a new model. In my own case it was two such occurrences.

The first one I'll cover in the afterword at the end of the book. Don't rush to it now and think you can skip the intervening pages and still get full value! By all means read it … but don't think that's all there is to it.

The second event, and the biggest gift I have ever received occurred in March 1999.

Here's how it unfolded...
A normally healthy, mid-thirties, average type of guy, on three recent occasions I had come out in an unexplained rash, or as the medics refer to it – giant urticaria. Like a heat rash which spread from head

to toe. Like an allergic reaction. But to what? Completely unexplained, completely random in its cause (that is, with no apparent link to food or any other trigger for the reaction), and completely frightening! The fourth instance was to have almost tragic consequences.

With Elizabeth, my wife, I was to meet a business acquaintance and her partner for lunch in Edinburgh. We parked the car, and walked the short distance to the restaurant in the west end of the city. We enjoyed a light lunch and great company before leaving the restaurant to head our separate ways. In fact, Elizabeth and I were to look for an eternity ring for her for our tenth wedding anniversary. In lighter moments of reflection, we often wonder whether the thought of me buying such a gift had anything to do with what happened next!

It began, as it had done on three occasions previously, with a tingling heat sensation on the back of my head, spreading to my ears, and from my hands, spreading up my arms, and from my belly spreading to my chest, waistline and groin. It happened in seconds. Uncomfortable. And so, time to get back to the car to drive home. Mild concern, rising to panic, as it just got worse … I guess because the quicker we walked back to the car, the quicker the reaction rushed round my system. By the time we had walked the three minutes back to the car, I could hardly see, as the rash had become a puffiness and my face began to swell … forehead, cheeks, neck, eyes.

I was really starting to struggle now. I could literally see the nerve endings in my eyeballs as I went snow-blind. We reached the car, and I slumped into the passenger seat. Frantically, Elizabeth started the car, and we were off. It would be a matter of relaxing, remaining calm, and soon it would be over … just like on previous occasions.

But somehow this was worse… and I knew it.

It already felt different. It wasn't subsiding, and I could feel that my breathing was starting to be affected. The eerie silence in which I was shrouded was the same silence I had experienced only once before when I had flown in a glider. As the cord from the towing cable releases and the drone of the towing aircraft becomes a distant memory, the aloneness has a unique soundlessness. And it was this soundlessness, not just silence, that I was experiencing now.

The blindness came over me like a white cloud, and the nauseating taste in my mouth told me I was going to pass out.

But it wasn't passing out. It was passing away.

At the moment my body slumped forward, my tongue swelled to fill my mouth, my mind went into overdrive and I knew for a split second that this was it! I was away! This must be how it ends.

What about the children? What about the love I wanted to give?

What about the things I hadn't seen, done, achieved yet?

What about all the things left undone?

When they say your life flashes before you. That's not true. It's your values that flash before you.

I felt myself stop breathing. And then I was gone.

I didn't even hear Elizabeth make the emergency call. Didn't hear her words.

Blue light. Flashing.

Strange hands. Voices… but distant.

Waking up on the pavement (I subsequently learned that it was several minutes later), with my body constrained on a stretcher, and a mask being put to my face was an incomprehensible shock.

What? A car crash? Is Elizabeth alright? What about the children? What happened?

No, mate … an anaphylactic shock they call it.

Since then, after numerous tests, no hint has been found as to the cause, or the trigger for the reaction. It has been over three years now … and every day, like many others who have suffered similar attacks, I have carried the epi-pen (an emergency adrenalin injector) with me in case of another severe occurrence.

They call it an anaphylactic shock. I call it my Light on the road to Damascus.

And that's a gift.

2

Guerrillas in Our Midst

Things left undone ...?

But I had worked hard – too hard?

Tirelessly – and never slackened. Always on some project or other. I had hobbies I thoroughly enjoyed (but didn't get as much time at as I wanted!). I had community involvement through my Round Table. I had time with my family. I had lots of friends, new and old. I had lots of lots.

So what else could be done? Why did I feel at that moment that I should be getting something more from life?

Over the next few hours, as I sat in that hospital bed in the Western General in Edinburgh, I couldn't think of anything else.

I have always been fascinated by what makes some people successful and others not. I had always been driven to success myself. I had always been 'motivated'. I had always tried hard at everything I had done – I think!

But, why hadn't I really hit the 'big time'. You know, really done what I wanted to do?

I thought, there must be a magic ingredient out there which some people have and others not. Either success is fated and there's nothing we can do one way or the other to change our lot in life, or there's a secret I'm not getting – and others are. But I had read lots of self-development books, listened to lots of audio tapes on the subject of success, and been to seminars and conferences where these themes abound.

Over the weeks that followed, I set out to define what the secret model could be. And the shocking thing was there was no secret. Most of what I learned appeared to be things which I, and doubtless many others, knew already.

But I did discover that there were a number of recurring themes which allowed those who were successful to do certain things, consistently, while others (though they might know what to do) were not taking action on these same things consistently. I decided to put together the jigsaw, and define the whole thing into a package which could be used by me, and easily passed on to others.

This book is what I discovered, uncovered and deduced from my observations, discussions, and some trial and error.

How the book is constructed

The easiest way to see the package as a whole, is to see it as a single diagram – the first of my 'Stratagrams' (I'll explain this term in a moment).

The core of the success system is Goals. This is the 'Counting Chickens' bit. This core (or sun) is orbited by the nine 'NEXUS Principles' (the 'making them hatch' bit!)

The whole model is in equilibrium. The principles operate in the light of the goals. They are all interconnected and held together by the pull of each other. The Vision, the Goals (Sun) are the source of all that matters. The absence of a Sun is the absence of matter. The absence of Reason. The Sun gives us our Reason to improve, to achieve, and to employ the principles. Without Reason, without Vision, without Goals, there can be no success.

17

The Success System

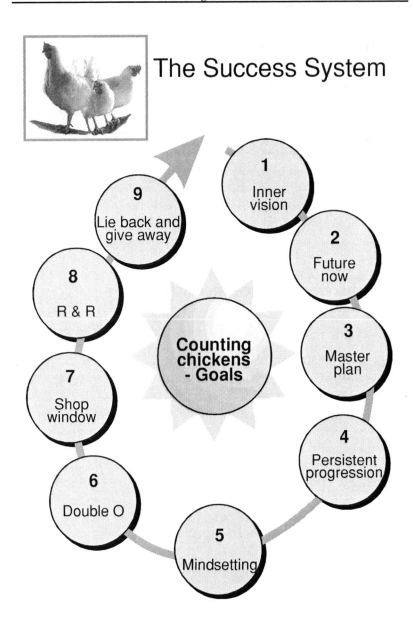

The NEXUS Principles – turning goal setting into goal getting

Guerrilla Tactics

Hearts and Minds

In unravelling the riddle of why some people succeed and others don't, it seemed to me that the first clue lies in another arena. An arena where effective performance and results mean the difference between life and death for the participants. One of the keys to success is the ability to become a 'Result-aholic' and as a template for this we are going to consider the similarities between business success in the modern world and the effectiveness of guerrilla warfare. This theme will help to frame many of the concepts we are going to cover in later chapters, but for now let's consider the correlation. And it's not just about business, don't forget. As individuals too, whether self-employed, employed, or employer, we can use this analogy to help understand how to be effective. So, everything I'm about to say about business applies equally to every facet of life. And guerrilla tactics work for teams and individual executives in large organisations and multinational companies also.

Guerrilla fighters have many parallels with the world of business because they have a cause or ideology at their core. This set of values coupled with a vision of what they ultimately want to achieve creates a higher ideal which compels them to extraordinary feats, often in what would seem to the 'regular soldier' as the most adverse conditions. The set of principles which they espouse creates a 'utopian' vision for the future and helps to generate the urgency and results focus needed to ensure they fight not just battles which are designed for individual victories, but which can only be seen as significant in the context of the whole campaign. And for business this is a key lesson – the importance of seeing each moment's activity as part of a whole campaign, rather than a set of unconnected actions or day-to-day routine.

For the guerrilla fighter, the higher ideal creates a Machiavellian instinct of the means focusing towards the ends. Note though the fine line difference between guerrilla forces and terrorists. Although terrorist tactics may be employed by guerrilla forces, the two are not necessarily one and the same. The guerrilla force which needs to work with the indigenous population and generate popular support must engage the 'Hearts and Minds' of the people. Indeed, the battle for the Hearts and Minds of our people (staff, customers, suppliers, supporters) will also be the true battleground in business. If we want to employ effective guerrilla tactics, we need to engage our people with a passion and enthusiasm which replaces the Rule of Terror which many companies slide towards.

We also need to recognise the importance of our own mindset in the whole equation. This is something to which we will be returning later.

Values and Rules

The adherence to a set of values has a distinct advantage for the Guerrilla Army and the modern business. There is a significant relationship between the need for a complex rule structure within an organisation and the value system in place. Consider a see-saw.

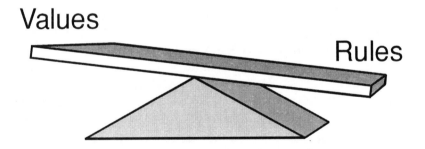

An organisation which is low on values will need to be high on rules in order for the people who make up the organisation to function effectively. And, because the rules can never be written to take account of every situation, the result is often a reliance on efficiency without any regard for effectiveness. An organisation which is high on values can afford to be low on rules – relying on the excellence of its people in doing the right things at the right time. Yes, there will need to be some rules and systems in place to smooth the whole process, but these should be there to allow people to use the fundamental abilities and values they have to couple with certain skills to obtain outstanding results – as with the Guerrilla fighter, who believes in the ideology, sees the vision, and knows when to set an ambush and when to simply 'lie up' in the jungle and wait to fight another day, and who also has the necessary skills required to do both effectively.

Opportunities and Problems

Consider the guerrilla fighter and the regular/conscript infantry soldier. When faced with dense jungle, monsoons, risk of illness and disease, a poor road network and difficult communication infrastructure, both adopt a significantly different approach. The latter will focus on a campaign which reflects the need to overcome these problems before engaging the enemy. The former will see these issues as advantages and opportunities to help win the war. They will employ the ambient conditions and environment, the climate and terrain, to best effect to win. They will ask 'what opportunity does fighting in the jungle provide?' Just as the British in Burma in World War Two were faced with these 'problems', the Japanese seemed able to use the conditions to generate a style of fighting which precipitated one of the speediest military advances in history. It was only when the Allies started to use guerrilla tactics through Orde Wingate's Chindits that they were able to fight on equal terms.

In our business world, indeed in our lives as a whole, what opportunities are we missing because we are viewing the whole campaign as a struggle with a problem orientation? How can we develop the 'Opportunity Focus' to ensure that the ambient conditions are an aid to our success rather than a hindrance?

In later chapters, we will look at a variety of techniques and tools which will enable you to convert what you initially see as Problems into Challenges, and ultimately into Opportunities. However, for now it's important simply to understand the difference in attitude which is generated both within yourself as business owner and your team of people when you have an opportunity mindset.

21

Now, I believe that the reason most people find it difficult to cultivate such an outlook in their businesses, in their lives, is that there is no vision, no ultimate ideal to work towards. Without this vision and a set of principles to work to, most people cannot make value-based decisions and therefore they avoid being proactive in utilising the environment and business climate to best advantage. One of the difficulties which business people face day to day is the inability to find time to plan and make meaningful strategic decisions which will have an impact on the results they are achieving. The outcome of this is that most never address their real opportunities and simply fight the struggle every day. There is no overview of the strategic plan for the business.

Many of you will be familiar with the good old SWOT analysis. What are our Strengths? What are our Weaknesses? What are our Opportunities? What are out Threats? All very well – I have spoken to many businesses who (after a period of searching through the 'Strategic Planning File'), can lay their hands on the last SWOT analysis they did – two years ago.

In order to expose the long term strategic opportunities and threats which exist in our business environment, it has been suggested that a PEST analysis also be conducted in relation to Opportunities and threats. What Political, Environmental, Social and Technological changes are on the horizon which will impact our business?

All great stuff, and no doubt very revealing for our plans. However, creating the Opportunity focus which we need comes much more from the compelling business vision and the underlying values than it does from an analysis of the anticipated journey. So too for the Guerrilla Army which remains adaptable and versatile so that the hidden opportunities and threats can be turned into advantage through results-focused action which is consistent with the ideology and the ultimate goal. As one business writer commented, Martin Luther King did not say 'I have a Critical Path schedule …'

Small is – effective

Just as a guerrilla force does not curl up and die in the face of a larger competitor/enemy, so too do we as small businesses need to ask the question, 'What opportunities does being a small business confer in this environment?' In fact, the guerrilla troops simply find new skills and a different kind of warfare to suit them. They learn to fight on their terms. They understand their Key Result Areas (more of which later) and focus on putting massive action into these, leaving the other stuff undone. They use surprise, hit-and-run, speed and stealth. In business, do we? How often do we really surprise/delight our customers? Do we really 'wow' them? Or are we fighting the same war as the bigger competitors? Do we fight on grounds which are a disadvantage to us? Or do we know how to wait until exactly the right time to market our goods in the right package (camouflage!) to our niche market? Do we use our powers of business intuition to say 'NOW!' when we instinctively know the time is right to act? Do we hit and run – decide, do, and move forward quickly. Or have we been hampered by a huge machine of rules/systems and self-imposed limitations?

I recently heard the advice given that someone was using Powerless Effort rather than Effortless Power in their golf swing! How true that the business guerrilla knows when, where, how and why to maximise the leverage of their power to give optimum effect. In the same way, the guerrilla army knows when and where it should fight, how it should fight, and why it is fighting in the first place.

And it's not just the ability to use guerrilla tactics which comes from having a smaller army. Other advantages are having a less complex Command & Control structure, ease of communication and, as a result, speed of making decisions and then turning those decisions into action on the ground.

Levers and Stratagrams

Returning to our 'success solar system', as you will see, we will be addressing a number of success principles – The NEXUS Principles. But I wanted to make them short, sharp, and to the point, so I have focused on the *levers* and *stratagrams* which you can use to convert these principles into action. Many of the ideas within the principles have been discussed and expounded elsewhere, by scientists, psychologists, business writers, coaches and consultants. I felt it better to concentrate on how to put it all into practice through a package which is easy to follow, and which has some very visually represented tools for action.

So, before we go any further, a word about Levers and Stratagrams.

The Levers and Stratagrams associated with each principle are your ready-to-use toolkit. They provide an easy point of access to the principles, so that you can build up the habitual use which will allow the principles to become your personal tenets and guidelines for everything you do.

- A **Lever** is a very simple idea which, when employed, will create proportionately greater results than the effort required for its use.

- A **Stratagram** will be a less familiar term to you, and as such needs more in-depth explanation. The fundamental reason why these *Strategic Diagrams* are so important is because so many of us find that seeing a concept explained visually is much preferable and more readily understandable. And we are all more likely to use those things we understand. The Stratagrams are also an ideal way to portray a practical tool and give you a format to help employing several tools from maybe two or three individual NEXUS principles at the same time. By all means develop your own – there are potentially limitless numbers of Stratagrams. Find those that suit your style and don't be put off if you can't draw. This is not about creating masterpieces. It's about creating supports and structures which allow you to function at the peak of effectiveness.

When developing Stratagrams I have found it a great way to engage both sides of the brain – using the **left (logical) side** to develop the process or structure needed and the **right (creative/emotional) side** to devise the powerful symbols and emotive words and pictures required to make the device a compelling one to use. In addition, I believe that these Stratagrams should simplify both the concept and the use of the concept. Therefore, they are very simple to use.

There is no doubt that the Stratagrams owe a lot to the world of mindmapping and the pioneering work of the likes of Tony Buzan, et al. However, I am always amazed at how many people say 'I get confused at mindmapping – I'm never sure where to start'. I am increasingly worried by the seemingly growing band of Mindmap conventions and rules peddlars giving the impression that you must go on courses, take several tutorials, and be steeped in mindmap methodology before you can use them. It seems to defeat the object of opening up a whole-brained approach to thinking, planning and idea development. Similarly, I have come across many who can mindmap an initial concept, but never use the mindmap as a tool in itself – as a point of future reference or as a tool for monitoring progress of, say, a project or marketing campaign. This is where Stratagrams can and should be used, to fill that gap between understanding the concepts behind the NEXUS principles and actually applying them to your day-to-day activity. You could, as I have done, use the Stratagrams as the tools which make up your working business plan. But a word of warning here – don't expect your Bank Manager to understand, let alone see value in, these things unless they are of the more open-minded and entrepreneurial school who can see beyond the pages of figures and projections which seem to dominate so many fledgling business plans.

Stratagrams provide a physical and tangible expression of some intangible concepts. The physical use of them means it's easier to adopt the principles as habits. They allow you to 'self-coach' because they are the manifestation of the use of a success principle. If you aren't actually physically applying the tools, can you say that you are really adopting the principles? Or, more likely, are you simply paying lip-service to them. And this lip-service is not out of disregard for the concepts, which as I have said you will find very simple. In fact, most business concepts and personal development concepts are very simple. Some would say that success is simple. And so it is. Note I didn't say 'easy', but simple.

Whenever we hear an idea which is very basic and seems 'logical' to us, we assume that because it appears obvious then we must be using it.

For example – Nokia mobile phones. That the marketing effort was centred on the ability to change the covers (and therefore to have different coloured phones, and even phones with football team, pop group, and other allegiances so clearly displayed) changed the whole industry. As well as a paradigm shift, a masterstroke. But so very basic. And some would say logical – in hindsight.

The realisation of where the market was for mobile phones, and the understanding of the product in the eyes of that market, as a fashion accessory rather than a phone, led of course to the introduction of removable coloured covers, which became the key to the market.

Indeed it is the simplicity which seems to confuse most people. We all have a natural tendency to complicate, and the bigger the issue the more complex we want to make it! So we often dismiss the simple success concepts (even though they ring true with us) and we fail to put these ideas into practice, preferring a more complex route on the grounds that it must be cleverer!

The fact that we understand the concept does not mean we will naturally work to it. In the cold light of a classroom many self-development ideas seem so straightforward. But putting them into practice is the critical bit. In the past, I have often been frustrated by self development and business development books, tapes and seminars which have a lack of real, useable, pragmatic tools. It's all very well to have a list of 101 Time Management tips, but until you too can turn them into a habit, where is the toolkit to support you? The Levers and Stratagrams are designed to fill that void, and offer you new tools to help build the habit of operating in a new way. After all, in business we will always default to habits. The Stratagrams and Levers will help to develop the habits. They will provide the focus which will move you from purely considering the principles to actually doing them, without having to consciously think about which Principle is being employed. They create the bridge between the Strategy/Concept/Principle and the everyday activity, giving you leverage to raise you to the level of performance which you want to achieve.

It may be that one Stratagram per principle is all that is needed for you to know that you have adopted the principle. As long as the

Stratagram is being used frequently as a key guerrilla tactic (frequently enough to be considered a habit), it's likely that you are applying that concept to other areas of your life and business. The trick is to find the one Stratagram or Lever which works for you, or to develop one specifically as a hybrid of the ones offered here which suits your own style of working and applies the principle in question to you.

The adoption of Stratagrams will, in itself, indicate that at least two principles are at work, because they lie at the core of all the Stratagrams – Principle 3 (Master Plan) and Principle 6 (Order and Organisation). Indeed, in addition, they almost always employ the support structures required under Principle 4 (Persistent Progression). And their regular usage implies Principle 8 (Rehearsal and Renewal) is at work.

Okay, back to being a 'result-aholic'.

What was the fundamental difference I was observing between those high achievers and those who don't quite make it, in any arena, but particularly in the world of business?

The lesson of a Boy Scout

Let me share with you a story about when I was a boy scout. Some of you may even be familiar with this scenario yourselves.

I remember getting my first badge. I had worked particularly hard to get this one particular badge because it was my first one. And when I achieved it, I was so excited as I rushed home clutching the bright yellow triangle of cloth. I was desperate to sew it on to my uniform sleeve.

In fact I was so excited, and so desperate to see it on the sleeve, that I decided to sew it on myself.

However, what I didn't realise was that to sew it on properly, I needed to sew it on from the inside. And in the end it looked awful, because I had just tacked it on the outside of the sleeve. So my excitement was dashed and I really felt so embarrassed the next time I was at the scout hall.

So what is the message?

Well that's what personal and business effectiveness is about. You see, you can't just tack it on the outside. It comes from within.

It starts from the inside.

Effectiveness and efficiency

What I have found with so many people in business is that too much focus is on *Techniques* – ways of becoming more efficient – techniques that are tacked on to the outside.

You see, there is a huge difference between *effectiveness* and *efficiency*. And it's a vital difference. In business, this translates as the difference between:

Doing things right and doing right things.

Most people are focusing on doing things right, whether or not those are the right things to be doing!

Many people end up being extraordinarily good at doing the wrong things! The key difference is that effectiveness is about direction. Efficiency is simply about moving fast.

So in order to consider whether or not we're being effective, we've first got to know what the direction is. You need to have a Vision of the Destination you are aiming for. I call this a Prime Vision.

And so, to the centre of the system – to the sun.

The bright light, the source of all energy, inspiration, power and focus – our Goals –

3

Chicken and Egg

What came first?

It's not simply the goals which make up the Vision, it's the Reason for having those goals, and the Values which underlie them, which make the Vision compelling. And they must be OUR reasons (not someone else's) which underpin the goals in order to make them something which we will want to stick to, commit to and follow through on. Not an exercise in annual target setting which so many businesses and individuals fall into the trap of using, thinking that will do for goal-setting for another year!

So, what are the reasons for going into business on our own, for example?

What did come first? The chicken or the egg? Well, in the context of business life, it is always a DESIRE for a business which comes first and that comes from a DESIRE FOR MORE LIFE. Indeed, whilst people set up their own businesses for a wide range of reasons, most decide they want their own business because of the freedom and control that it will give them. FREEDOM and CONTROL. It's interesting that these are the two elements which most people in business feel that they don't have enough of.

Before you think we're getting a bit deep here, bear with me.

So, it's the *realisation of the need for more life* which comes first. It's an understanding of what a business can give you that will determine your perspective on the business at key moments later on. This understanding of your business being designed as a life-giver rather than a life-taker, as a tool of personal freedom rather than a 'ball and chain', as a source of control rather than a restrictor, is always present in the most successful entrepreneurs. And to a greater or lesser degree, that is the vision which makes it worthwhile having a business in the first place.

Whilst all business people hold this vision dear (in varying degrees) at the outset, it's only those who can maintain the vision and understand the values it brings who will reap those benefits of FREEDOM and CONTROL. For many, however, the business will become the very thing which takes away those two 'golden eggs'. Those people become slaves to the business. In fact, they haven't got a business at all. Instead they have simply created self-employment. Not a business, but a job for themselves. And there is a difference.

And please, please remember – I'm not just talking about setting up and running a business here. I'm using the small business as a prime example of a major goal in life. This applies to YOU, whatever your role, whatever your business, and whether you are employer, self-employed or indeed an employee. We are all Chief Executive of ourselves. We are all entrepreneurs of our own lives.

'Whether you like it or not, you are the author of your own life story.'

This phrase had a profound effect on me the first time I read it, and it set me thinking. Yes, of course, we should be seeing ourselves as script writers. In doing so, we claim a sense of personal responsibility, and a sense of control. And a sense of freedom. Looking forward to the unfolding of our story, a story which we are writing for ourselves, creates eager anticipation and excitement at what the next instalment might be, as well as making sense of the current instalment, and putting past instalments into perspective. This whole approach of seeing yourself as writer of your life story also raises some deeper questions. Are you writing a story to be proud of? Are you genuinely looking forward to the next episode? What is the next chapter? This is your own soap opera – but it's genuine and real.

And this is another factor which seems to set apart the most successful entrepreneurs, their almost 'you-only-live-once-so-make-it-count' approach to their lives – a sense of their fragile mortality which drives them to take effective and speedy action where others would stall. Many see their business journey as an adventure story, with themselves as authors of this one-off tale, orchestrators of their destiny. So, if you are embarking on your own business venture, or indeed if you are in business but have never thought in that way before, put the business into the context of what it can provide you with – as a tool for the other facets of your life.

One of my favourite moments in the film *Apocalypse Now* involves the phrase 'If is the middle word in Life'. We spend our whole lives dealing with ifs. But in business, too many are afraid to make assumptions, create ifs, count chickens. In fact, having a dream is positively discouraged as 'unrealistic' or 'getting ahead of ourselves' by those people who are closest, in business terms, to the would-be entrepreneur at the outset. The result is a failure to create a compelling vision for the business.

The fundamental skill of creating an engaging image of the finished business 'product' is glossed over by most business advisers, and paid meagre attention by potential backers. For most business owners, it is a skill never to be explored or to see the light of day on paper. It is merely stored as a vague hope masquerading as a 'business goal' somewhere in the archives of the mind.

It is the Vision of the finished business, expressed without fear of eggs not hatching, which needs to fuel the business strategy. This business strategy revolves around satisfying the 'ifs'. Without the vision, there can be no strategy or plan. And without the plan, the central 'if' falls out of the business owner's life. Satisfying the ifs in the Vision is what business strategy is about. The assumptions form the strategy for success. The ability to constantly ask the question 'what if we could do …?' keeps a business growing. Because most people will not develop the courage to admit the assumptions even to themselves for fear of ridicule, rejection or 'failure', they do not create the success vision, and therefore don't plan. Planning naturally involves designing a set of actions which will lead to a given result.

Without a design for this result, most business plans become an exercise in mathematics, formulated in a void, and voided on the first day of business when the shop doors open and 1.01% more (or fewer) of the projected customers arrive clutching their cash and wanting to partake of your goods or services.

Many of the 'ifs' of a business plan are made at a subconscious level anyway, being the fruits of our mindset, beliefs, experiences and perceptions. So why not add enough ifs into the plan to create a hugely desirable outcome, something which will excite to action and not just a once-visited exercise to encourage potential lenders to back your project?

Big Bang – an idea is born

So you have a great business idea? Really?

One of the most interesting facets of being asked to address groups on goal-setting is that those people in employed positions always put down that running their own business would be one of their life's ultimate desires. And, guess what – most of the 'business owners' put down that they would simply love a nine-to-five number !

You will have had countless conversations like this yourself.

'Oh, yes – I've got a great idea for a business. We could do this ... and that ... and all we'd need is this ... and one of those ... and off we go ... '

So, off you go, then. But why is it that so few people do go off and run their own business? And why is it that fewer still really create anything like the personal freedom and control that was the purpose of setting up in business in the first place. Well, partly it's that failure to recognise the difference between setting up and running a business and becoming self-employed which I mentioned earlier.

But let's consider what often happens to make people take that 'risk' of setting up for themselves.

Normally they will have been forced by one or other of the following:

- made redundant
- fed up with current job so 'I'll go and do it for myself' – normally as a result of a personality clash with line manager.

And for those who do take the plunge and do make it work we hear the time-honoured 'I wish I'd done it years ago.'

The reason they didn't do it years ago (and why so few, proportionately, of those who think about it do it at all) is that there was no necessity. And we all know that necessity is the mother of invention. She is also the mother of getting on with things. It's amazing how all procrastination can be decimated by the arrival of necessity.

But hold on a minute – if you are going to do it purely out of necessity, your business is being set up doomed to failure. Or at least failure in the sense of not achieving true potential – true freedom and control.

Let me explain. If you needed necessity to make you embark on the whole adventure, then it is highly likely that you will continue to operate so close to the necessity line that you will always feel comfortable as long as you are just above break even – and that's where you'll aspire to stay! So you'll have a business which provides a subsistence existence, and nothing like the freedom and control which are the cornerstones of a truly great business. You are, in effect, setting yourself up to – er, get by – and only that.

So here's a test you can apply to your great business idea:

Ask yourself, 'If I had the cushiest, most comfortable nine-to-four job with holidays and a benefits package to make anyone green with envy, would I still want to go for this business idea?'

If the answer is a resounding 'YES', then it's likely you are going into business with the right perspective, even if mother necessity is, in reality, playing a part.

Golf without holes

Life without goals – is like golf without holes.

Many people say, 'oh, I don't need to write goals ...' Fine.

And many people like to play golf for the walk, fresh air, companionship, exercise and so on, and in effect the holes are largely immaterial, and the score is immaterial.

BUT – don't complain if, deep down, you want to be a Championship golfer, or if you're not improving to where you want to be – i.e. don't say, 'I'm not as successful as I'd like to be – ' if you haven't set goals.

And don't look at others and say, 'I would love to be like that ...'

You must be prepared to put holes on the course. Something to measure by and something to aspire to and beat, something to set as a challenge to give you a reason to improve performance. How else do you know what the score is ...?

A number of years ago, at a seminar, I heard the startling story of the Harvard study. This took place in 1952 and consisted of a survey in which all the graduates that year were asked a series of lifestyle and expectation questions. Part of the survey was about goals. The research showed that of all the students in that graduating class:

- 87 per cent had no goals whatsoever
- 10 per cent said they had goals, but that they were not written down
- 3 per cent said that they had written goals for their life ahead.

The most astounding part of the study was what came next. Twenty years later in 1972, the same people were asked a series of lifestyle questions. What was revealed was that the 3 per cent who had written goals in 1952 were more financially successful than the other 97 per cent put together!

Okay – so money is not a measure of success. And that's not the point of the study. What it does reveal, however, is that there is a correlation between having goals, a point of focus and our ability to move further ahead than otherwise. The story of this survey has passed into personal development folklore.

So, I decided to test the figures. Not scientifically, perhaps. But whenever I ask the question of any group of people, either at seminars or workshops, or whenever I ask it of individuals I am coaching, (regardless of social class, upbringing, job, or any other factor), I have found the same.

87 percent have no goals, and 10 percent have 'unwritten' goals, and 3 percent have written goals.

Remember those figures – 87 percent, 10 percent, 3 percent.

They will crop up again later in the book.

Why writing goals is so important

A client challenged me during a recent group coaching session and asked why it was so important to have goals written down. He wasn't against the concept of having goals – we all know their importance (though research, as we have seen, suggests that only 3 percent have goals, written and with clear strategies for their accomplishment). So why have them written?

You will have your own answer to that. For me, it's about committing personally to the goals. And, a better question might be 'why shouldn't you write them down?' In other words, what possible advantage could be gained by not writing them down? I am convinced that one of the real reasons people don't set goals is they either don't know how to (i.e. the method), they are frightened to (fear of failure, or fear of success!), or they don't recognise the importance of goals, or that they aren't really committed to the goal (i.e. it's not really a goal at all).

So it's important to write our goals down. But how? Well the exercises and stratagrams throughout this chapter are designed to help you get your visions and goals onto paper. The important thing to remember is that the writing of our goals should make them compelling, and exciting to us. They must be so powerful that we can't wait to get out of bed in the morning and get moving. They must drive us to breakthrough levels of performance and immense enjoyment of our lives. If you don't believe me, look at what Steven Spielberg, the most famous and successful film director of the modern age, has to say:

'I wake up so excited, I can't eat breakfast!'

So it's imperative we use superlative adjectives to describe the achievement of these goals. Setting out to 'lose a little weight and get a little healthier' sounds an awful lot better, and more exciting, if we say instead that we have a vision of a fantastic body, immense levels of energy, and oozing confidence.

When setting your goals, and in particular when designing your Prime Vision, remember we are not looking at how you are going to get there yet. This is planning. And I know that many people and companies get the two confused and end up setting plans, not goals. The planning is – how you are going to get there? And that comes later.

To illustrate the point, consider the traditional approach to setting strategy and my alternative. As you will see from this, the whole approach becomes very different. We set the goals and visions in terms of what we want to achieve as a quantum leap forward, not in terms of what we have achieved so far, which by its very nature could be a limitation on what we believe we can achieve, and therefore a limitation on our expectations in terms of performance and results.

The traditional, 5-stage strategic approach	A different approach
• Where are we now? • How did we get here? • Where do we want to get to? • What are the barriers and obstacles? • What are we going to do to overcome the barriers and move to where we want to be?	• Where do we want to get to? (vision) • Why do we want to get there? • Where are we now? • What are the barriers and obstacles? • What are we going to do to overcome the barriers and move to where we want to be?

The Magnificent Seven

Now for an exercise to set your mind racing and to start to define your direction. This is a great way to expand the levels of expectation and set out a template for what you really want from life. It is interesting how so many people are set business targets, but very few have these targets set in the context of the overall direction of life. It's imperative that the Prime Vision represents a balance of what we really want from life.

If you don't intend to do this exercise just now, skip the next 7 pages. Don't read the questions and then come back and answer them at a later stage. It's important that you are working on gut-feeling and instinct to get the most from this exercise.

The exercise comprises seven questions and will take a little over five minutes to complete. All you need is a clear head, and a pen. There's room on each page for you to write the answers. Ensure you are away from any potential interruptions.

Don't worry if you are unable to answer any of the questions. If you have a mental block, or the question simply catches you so off guard that you can't even think, leave it blank. That fact may, in itself, tell you something about your current direction and goals.

It is important you write as much down as possible in answering each question, and the crucial factor in getting the most from this is to always go with your gut-feeling. Don't contrive your answers.

Ready? Here goes ...

The Magnificent Seven

Question One
One minute only to answer this question.

What are your <u>five</u> most important values in life?

Now put them in priority order (15 seconds)

The Magnificent Seven

Question Two
30 seconds to answer this question.

What are your <u>three</u> most important goals right now?

(If you cannot think of three, simply decide which you would desire most, right now - more time, more money?)

The Magnificent Seven

<u>Question Three</u>
One minute to answer this question.

Describe what you would do with your time, if you
were given only six more months to live,

The Magnificent Seven

<u>Question Four</u>
One minute to answer this question.

If you won £4million on the lottery, how would you spend that money, and what would you do with your life?

The Magnificent Seven

<u>Question Five</u>
30 seconds to answer this question.

Looking back over your life so far, what things have you been doing when you have had the greatest feeling of personal achievement, self-fulfilment and success?

The Magnificent Seven

Question Six
30 seconds to answer this question.

What one thing would you love to do, if you could overcome your fear?

The Magnificent Seven

<u>Question Seven</u>
30 seconds to answer this question.

If there were a magic wand for your life, which meant that you could be, do or have anything you wanted, what would you wish for, knowing you couldn't fail?

Although I have altered them a little, I first encountered this set of questions when listening to an audio tape by the American business and sales guru, Brian Tracy. For me they came at just the right time. I hope they have for you too!

The Goals Hierarchy

Prime Vision

In our success solar system, if the nine NEXUS principles represent the planets, it is our goals (with our Prime Vision at the core) which represent the sun. They are at the centre of success. The equilibrium of the whole success system is maintained by these goals. And in particular the **Prime Vision** which not only relates to a specific single achievement, but also our fundamental values. And most goal setting exercises forget to underpin the whole with Values. Which is

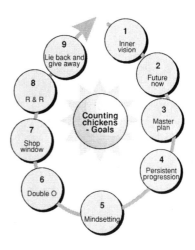

why so many people do not buy into the goals they set themselves.

Over the years, I have discovered much discussion and disagreement about whether goals should be SMART goals or 'Shoot for the Moon' goals. If this has passed you by, perhaps I can explain. On the one hand, there are those who say that goals should be SMART – Specific, Measurable, Achievable, Realistic, Timed. A useful mnemonic, and one which has entered household vocabulary (or certainly training room vocabulary). But there are others who say that Goals set as Achievable and Realistic will by their very nature limit our performance because they do not stretch us beyond the outer limits of our comfort zone. Their suggestion is that we must think big and shoot for the highest goal. That way, we'll achieve beyond the level we would have achieved otherwise. Go for the stars and at least you'll reach the moon.

Both arguments have their merits, but let me help to unravel the confusion. I believe that whilst both camps are using the same word, the 'Goals' they refer to are in fact very different in their nature. Again this relates to the confusion between setting goals and planning how to achieve. These two activities whilst not entirely divorced, do require very different approaches. Whilst our Prime Vision should be of the Shoot for the Moon variety, the SMART version could apply to shorter term objectives or tasks – which I refer to as Tactical Targets and Special Missions. But even these should remain stretching in scale otherwise the true value of the targets is lost.

Targets are there not just to measure performance and results, but more importantly, to enhance performance and results.

So your Prime Vision will link Values (state of life/living – i.e. a lifestyle) with your vision of the material life you want and the vision of your 'finished' business (which is the tool to allow you to have the life).

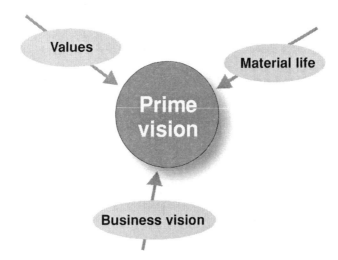

This Prime Vision allows you to articulate 'What I stand for is ...'

It is because of the need for the inclusion of values in this that our gut-feeling vision is very powerful. Indeed it is essential that we call upon this resource to create the Prime Vision. And this is where we Count Chickens!

Seeing is believing – and believing is seeing.

We can only achieve what we can believe. *Counting Chickens* is about creating a vision which is so compelling that it sends ripples of expectation and commitment to the cause throughout your every day.

Once you see with such clarity, you can't help but believe. And once you believe so wholeheartedly, you can't help but achieve.

Seeing = believing
Believing = seeing

We can only achieve what we can believe.

Therefore, in order to achieve, we must first SEE

So, what is your destination? What is *your* Prime Vision?

I find it incredible how so few people have a Prime Vision in life.

What is interesting is that for those who do have a Prime Vision, the impact it has on their business direction is phenomenal. It allows them to put business into perspective and balance with the rest of their life. And it allows them to be effective.

Time Travelling Exercise

Time to count some chickens

There is a problem with many goal setting tools in that they are not compelling enough and they also rest within a framework of the Present. In other words, people and businesses simply do not imagine the future – they set goals for now, working within the current framework and environment. They don't travel forward, picture the future and place themselves in it.

Let's do an exercise which will allow you to put yourself firmly in the future.

If you are sitting down as you read this, first understand that you are currently grounded in ……… (date), say April 2003.

Now, move your chair forward about 9 inches. Imagine you are now in 2008. It's been a brilliant five years, and you are now in the position of having the life and business you always wanted to have. Close your eyes and picture it. Okay, so you can't read with your eyes closed – so read to the end of this bit, and then come back to do it!

Ask yourself the magic wand question

If a magic wand had been waved and the business had been transformed into exactly what I wanted it to look like, what would that be?

And not just the business. If a magic wand had been waved and my life had been transformed into exactly what I wanted it to be, what would that look like?

Create as much detail as you can. Speak out loud about how it looks and feels to be in 2008 and things being absolutely fantastic. What would be your dream vision? Go on – describe it. If you have a partner you can share this with, have a conversation set in April 2008 where you are describing to him or her all the great things that have happened to bring you to the fabulous position you are now in. Really Be There!

That's how to count chickens. And the more detail you can picture, the more compelling the vision becomes.

Okay, so imagine that instead of five years ahead, you had actually got there in three years – because it's amazing what you can really achieve if you are focused and set your mind to it.

Time travel	**New date** _____

Infinite Boundary

Notes on the Stratagram

So far, we have mentioned setting quantum goals on several occasions in the preceding pages. The fact is that the human potential is far greater than we often realise, and often when we set our goals we don't think big enough.

This stratagram is devised deliberately to expand the mindset and raise expectations so that you can truly set a vision which is at a quantum level. This helps to remove any self-imposed limitations, raises the bar of possibility to an (until now) unimagined level.

Once we have challenged our mind with that expansion, we find it almost impossible to shrink back.

We have therefore created a huge leap forward in our beliefs about what we really want to set as a goal, and, yes, it's a huge leap forward, a leap of faith, first created in our mind's eye.

Simply follow the two steps on the stratagram, and you will see what happens.

The Lifemap

You are now at the stage where you can produce a Lifemap (see page 52). This is a one-page snapshot of all the things you want to achieve in all areas of your life. Making it diagramatic, and including as much colour as possible enables you to use it as a vivid, inspiring injection when you need it. It should be revisited on a regular basis, and updated.

Once you have this snapshot, you can then write each individual goal in full, separated into the six headings.

The six key areas will encompass sub-areas which will involve certain goals you want to achieve (e.g. places you want to visit in the 'travel' section).

The Infinite Boundary

Step One

Describe on this side of the boundary what you would see as such an impossible dream for your business vision and your life. Put as much detail as possible.

Step Two

Describe the vision one step back from the boundary. Almost impossible, and a considerable stretch in imagination. Concentrate on the results of the vision - i.e. what it gives you to be there.

The Lifemap

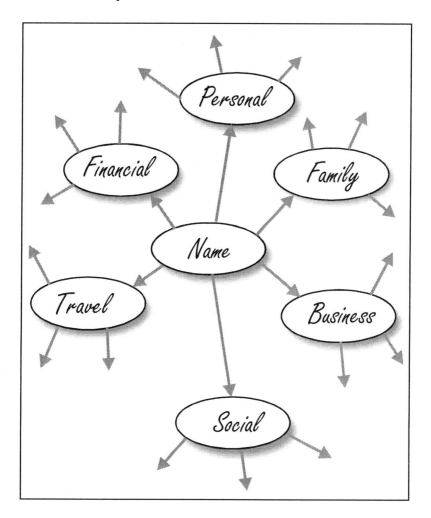

Strategic Objective

So if you were to draw a mountain, representing your business vision:

● What is the SUMMIT about for you?

- What does it look like from up there?
- What does it feel like to be there, at the top?

And from where you are currently standing at the foot of the mountain, where on the mountain is Base Camp – i.e. that point at which you have got your act together so much that you are able to really start the exciting ascent to the top. Let's call this our Strategic Objective.

What knowledge, skills, regular activity, and structures need to be in place in your Base Camp toolkit. And from here at the foot of the hill, how are you going to reach that point. Which particular foothills are you going to start on? (See the 'On the Mountain' Stratagram later in this chapter.)

This Base Camp is our business strategic objective. The finished article. Again, not SMART (Specific, Measurable, Achievable, Realistic, Time-bound) as that would be self-limiting – but SMT. This should represent a quantum leap forward for the business. Unless it is a quantum leap, it will not be compelling enough to create massive improvements in performance. It needs to be exciting - something to get out of bed in the morning for!

The 19th Century, the Prussian military strategist, Von Clausewitz, pointed out that there is no single formula for winning a war. Even if the general begins with a campaign plan, the battle itself will force a change in strategy because its exact outcome cannot be predicted. The next steps beyond each contact with the enemy will have to be assessed based on the position at that time, and the plan built from there. But the overall Strategic Objective, and the Prime Vision of embarking on the war in the first place remains constant. And in business, conditions are constantly changing, of course. So we need to have several strategies which we can adopt quickly as circumstances change – but always consistent with the Prime Vision and the Strategic Objective.

A Strategic Objective is not a huge, lengthy action plan, therefore. It's a clearly identified point in the future which we want to reach. The action plans are made up of the Tactical Targets and Special Missions which we adopt along the way.

Back at the chicken theme ...

If we were pulling a wishbone for your business, and you won, what would you wish for?

Write down the first thing that comes into your head, as often it's our gut-feeling which tells us so much about what we know deep down we should be doing to achieve success – and this is usually a key element in building to the Strategic Objective.

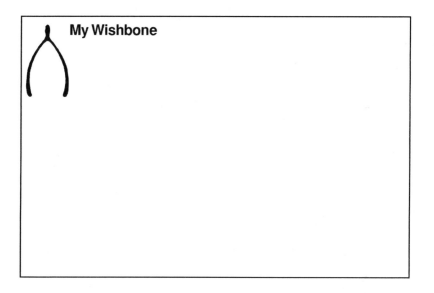

My Wishbone

'On the Mountain'

This is a tool to capture the link between the Strategic objective and the Business Vision – or the Prime Vision and the Business Vision. It can be used for any major goal, however. And as well as with businesses, I have used it on many occasions when coaching employed executives who want to progress their careers to new heights.

The challenge for most people is that when setting long term goals, in business and in the personal arena, they make the mistake of starting from now and working forward in stages to where they want to be in say 3, 5 or 10 years.

But, as we have shown, for goal setting to be effective in

supercharging performance and improving results, it is much better to create a compelling vision by leaping forward to the end result, and then building backwards. This is the way a mountaineer would design an expedition or a Field Marshal plan a military campaign.

Start by describing in detail the end product, the final vision of what you want to achieve. Only after this is done should you be considering How to get there through setting goals working backwards in stages.

In this case, project yourself to the top of the mountain and describe in detail what it looks and feels like to be at the top. Use as many superlative adjectives as possible to describe the success you have achieved and what it means to your whole life.

- *Write this in the box at the right of the summit.*

Then, knowing where you want to get to, decide what Base Camp needs to be for you. In other words, base camp is that position at which all the skills and capabilities are in place to make a launch at the summit. I have found that this Base Camp toolkit should be broken down into 4 areas – Knowledge, Skills, Activity, Structure (or systems). This goes for whether you are running your own business or whether you want to move up a career mountain.

- *Add these details to the boxes at the Base Camp level.*

Working back from this Base Camp (which is in essence a shopping list for your development), decide on the First Steps.

- *Write them down in the lowest box – and commit to them.*

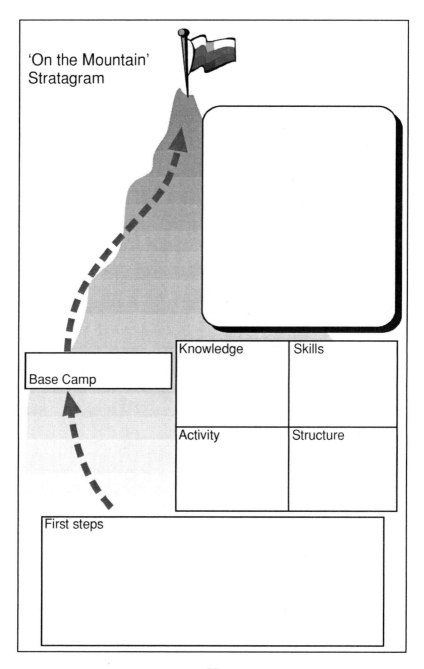

'On the Mountain' Stratagram

Base Camp

Knowledge	Skills
Activity	Structure

First steps

Tactical targets

These are the large and significant steps towards the make up of the Strategic Objective.

They represent significant way-points to be reached. They can often be set as annual targets, or even shorter term objectives – perhaps over 90 days, which I have found to be a timescale in which a lot can be achieved if the targets are set well. And it is a long enough timescale for you to be adventurous and ambitious in the goals you set.

Referring to your Lifemap gives you the template for these targets. They should reflect the 6 key areas of your life in order to ensure a balance. In a purely business context, they should reflect the growth of the business across all areas in the same way. Again, write them out and keep them prominent and refer to them often.

Awesome Special Missions (ASMs)

These are shorter term Breakthrough projects which unlock specific doors to lead to your tactical targets and strategic objective.

'Projects' is too dull a word for me, I'm afraid, which rekindles images of third year history or geography lessons. Projects reflects an academic and sedentary approach which I wanted to banish from my own approach to business breakthroughs. ASMs are *awesome* because they represent the accomplishment of stretching goals and significant feats. They are special because we want the whole team to look back on them in years to come and say, 'Do you remember when we did x-y-z ...' And they are *missions* because they engage our hearts and minds. We must be compelled to achieve them. We must draw on all our resources to achieve them – like military operations on a raging battlefield; like the enemy machine-gun bunker which must be taken out; like the hostage siege which must be broken. No place for faint hearts, or long-drawn-out meetings to think about, pontificate, postulate on what must be done next. Once the start line has been crossed, it's all action. And all productive action. This is about overcoming major challenges, achieving speedy and effective breakthroughs. We will return later in the book to look at some specific tools which you can use in relation to ASMs.

'Man with no target hit nothing.'

In all of this, remember that the goals themselves are not the objective – it is what the achievement of the goals will give us that is the objective. The goals themselves are simply tools to improve performance and results. As in chess, where the ultimate goal of 'capturing the King' is the Prime Vision, there are lots of optional strategies and tactical targets along the way. The end vision does not change. But the strategies will alter along the way. The ability of the entrepreneur and business person to speedily adapt from one tactical target or strategic objective to another is critical. But it does not mean that you avoid having those set in the first place. Yes, they may be overtaken by events. And you will need to be flexible to change. But that does not detract from their invaluability as tools to foster supercharged performance and dynamic results along the way.

And one of the most significant results of having goals at all levels is that they remove barriers to performance. Many people think that in order to improve performance, new skills and techniques must be taught. But this brings us back to the boy scout analogy. Putting new techniques on the outside. No! Peak performance comes from utilising the true talents and abilities which are normally masked by the barriers we encounter daily. In the same way that, faced with a crisis, people are able to perform feats which would normally be beyond their wildest imagination, so too in business, we are compelled to perform extraordinarily when we have clear objectives and a compelling vision (reason) to do so. The lady who, following a car accident, is able to lift the vehicle off her beloved child who is trapped underneath is all the evidence we need that we can be effective beyond the limits of our imagination when compelled. Suddenly the barriers to performance are gone.

Give 4X for your Goals

This Stratagram will help you to make your goals more compelling because it takes you beyond the goal itself to the Reason for wanting to achieve the goals.

Many people decide on goals without generating enough desire and reason behind the goal, and because the goals are therefore not compelling enough, the enthusiasm wanes.

- Start by writing the goal in the central circle.
- Then using different coloured pens, answer the questions shown.

Asking the four questions shown and listing the answers in the appropriate spaces will be a valuable point of reference to keep up your persistence later on! It also helps to clarify whether you are really serious about the goals in the first place.

Give 4X for your goals

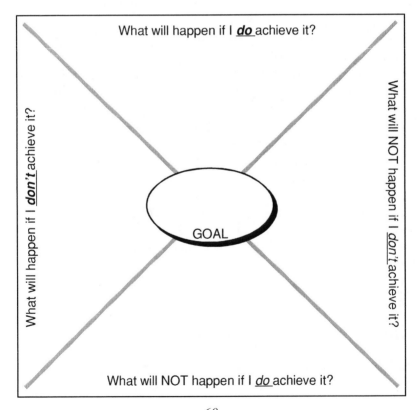

What will happen if I ___do___ achieve it?

What will happen if I ___don't___ achieve it?

What will NOT happen if I ___don't___ achieve it?

GOAL

What will NOT happen if I ___do___ achieve it?

Go on – Count those Chickens

How many times have you heard the sceptics say:

'Never assume – or you make an Ass out of U and Me!' with a degree of self satisfaction which only comes with years of practice in the art of negativity.

You see, we are constantly assuming. We are constantly dealing in Ifs. Making the Ifs happen is bringing the plan to fruition. But we need to have the Ifs to start with.

By contrast, where many people feel comfortable making assumptions, is in dealing with the bigger questions.

So, don't assume that you have all the time in the world to build your business empire. You don't. In fact, getting to grips with the fragility of your own existence and your insignificance in the grand scale of things can be an extremely valuable ally in the mindset of the successful business person.

Why is it that so many of the 'Ass out of U and Me' Brigade are quite prepared to assume they have got an eternity to do the things they say they want in life. You haven't. So stop assuming you have.

' A lot of what we ascribe to luck is not really luck at all.
It's seizing the day and accepting responsibility for your future.
It's seeing what other people don't see
and pursuing that Vision.
Howard Schultz – Starbucks

Remember...

The goals you set are simply tools for enhancing performance and improving results.

'The Greatest danger for most of us is
Not that our aim is too High and we Miss it,
But that it is too Low and we Reach it.'
Michelangelo

Time to Download:

Remember – 'To know and not to do, is not to know!'

This is not a chance just to write down things that have been confirmed, but more importantly new things that have been learned.

Action Zone

What I have learned so far ...

What I am going to do about it/use from now on ...

Section Two

'The NEXUS Principles'

4

Blockbusters

? What makes successful people successful?

? Do they know they are doing it?

? Are they consciously using any tools which others aren't using?

? Are they subconsciously better equipped for success?

? Is it all down to luck or can you deliberately create habits of success?

? At the point at which a composer lays down the final notes in his masterpiece, does he know it's a masterpiece – or is he just doing his best to do a good job? All in a day's work!

These are the questions with which I have wrestled over the years, and which you yourself may frequently ask.

I am not going to embark on a discussion over the definition of 'success', since as you will undoubtedly have already thought, it's different things for different people.

But the underlying precursor to any success, is goals. Even if the only goal you have is to enjoy every moment, stress free, with no pressure. That's a goal – and a very worthy one – and also very difficult to achieve!

It has been said that in the field of personal development therefore, 'success is Goals, and all else is purely commentary.'

So, perhaps, as we have set tackled the goals element in section one when counting our chickens, here is the commentary – the way to get them to hatch.

But it's not just a commentary on achieving future goals. It's also a commentary on enjoying the journey and making it a meaningful trip. Indeed, enjoying the journey should be an essential part of all your goals anyway, and certainly will be fundamental to the Prime Vision you develop. Enjoying the journey will result only when values and goals are linked.

Let me ask you this. If you had a jigsaw puzzle, with all the pieces scattered in front of you on a table, and all of those pieces were blank white, how difficult would it be to put the jigsaw together? Of course, virtually impossible.

What we must realise is that it's the pattern on the pieces which creates the clues. That is the difference. And most people have all of the pieces for their life's success in front of them. But they do not see (or are not looking for) the pattern. Most people are born with all of the fundamental abilities which will make them successful. And for many, it's the sudden dawning that all the pieces ARE there which makes the difference. We often need to realise that the answer was in our hands all along.

The breakthrough came for me when I started to observe those things about my own actions which lead to a desired outcome. And then to tally them with those things that others were also doing to achieve their own desired outcomes. I then considered all the things I wasn't doing and which others were doing to be effective. And through trial and error, I began to use them myself. This showed me that it was their use of a tool or technique or an effectiveness habit which was the difference, and not that they were any different than anyone else, or more knowledgeable, or more skilful necessarily. It was the way they approached the use of their resources, the way they thought, their apparently-natural style and habits which made the difference.

Indeed, I observed, and I am sure you have too, that most people in business, in life, when looking for improvement, know most of the things they should be doing. Most people know what they should do in order to stop smoking, lose weight, get more business and sales, improve the quality of the time they invest with their families and loved ones, improve the quality and conduct of their business meetings, improve the way they lead or manage others. And so on. Most people are not floored by some blinding technique or skilful trick. They know what to do.

The difficulty is in doing it, consistently. This is the real challenge. Most people have a series of blockers and barriers. And often it's the same blocker which gets in the way of everything. It is a recurring theme time and again, in a whole life story of unfulfilled ambitions.

Those who are successful, on the other hand, appear to find a way through, over, or around the barriers. They have blockbusting traits which they employ, mostly without thinking. So the principles had to relate to **how to 'Block-Bust'**

I began to realise that in essence these factors for success could be broken down into only a very few principles. And I wanted to make it easy for me to refer to these principles in inspiring myself, and self-coaching, and then know that they could be adopted by everyone. In other words, I wanted to find a set of principles which employed a set of tools which would work in any environment to achieve success. The NEXUS principles are just that package.

Before I go into the package, a few notes about NEXUS.

To many people, the film Bladerunner is more than just a science fiction thriller. Here is a brief outline.

Harrison Ford plays the part of a special 'BladeRunner' agent whose role is to track down and destroy (retire) androids known as replicants. These androids are the product of years of genetic research and engineering such that they are now so advanced that they have become virtually superhuman in the later models. The codename for the models is NEXUS and the latest version is NEXUS 6 – a highly intelligent form, and one in which even human memories and emotions have been replicated. These androids have, however, been encoded with a 'shelf life' (based on their incept date) in order to limit them to performing certain tasks over a set lifetime. The replicants have become so intelligent that they now are desperate to find out when their time is due to expire. They have emotions now, and like humans, they are preoccupied with their lifespan.

One of the key elements which preyed on my mind when watching the film for the first time was the whole concept of the search for 'more life.' The fact that the Androids (Replicants) are so desperately preoccupied with their plight and the contrast with the humans who have become emotionally disengaged and unconcerned with such big issues struck a chord. So I wanted to create a package of success tools which would help anyone achieve 'more life' – both craving more of what life can give us, and also what was being achieved in life. And in particular, I wanted to apply these to a business context – especially in the context of the freedom and control which all business people desire. Because, we too all have an 'incept date' and a shelf life. We are all running a Time Bank Account – and there is no overdraft facility on the account. We never get a statement telling us how much is left in there either. Perhaps this is why those people who have come close to death have developed a heightened awareness that they are writing their own life story. But, you don't need to have had a near death experience to become successful!

The value in these principles and their associated toolkit, the Levers and Stratagrams, is that whether you are a business owner, self-employed, or an employee, there is immense value and relevance in their usage. They have been used by many people, in many roles over the past few years, and many people have adapted them and given me immense feedback on alternative applications, which has allowed me to refine them until I know they work. Every time.

The NEXUS principles emerged not so much as a set of values, but as guiding tenets and thought patterns which would allow me and others to structure our success through a set of habits and regimes. And a recurring theme is that in life, in business, people always default to habit. Which is why a lot of training and development work which organisations embark upon doesn't work. It focuses too much on newly imposed disciplines without underpinning it with the structures required to turn those disciplines into habits. The NEXUS principles are therefore a set of easy to employ guidelines and concepts. The tools, Levers and Stratagrams, are easy to employ actions which result form the principles. They are the means of employing these principles.

The principles are definitely to be seen as a set. They are of themselves individually no great shakes. They may, in fact, appear a little simplistic and most people when they first hear the principles think 'Oh, well, yes. I already do that,' because they appear to be such logical concepts. Although on its own a principle may seem almost too easy to need any effort to use, still consider the individual Levers and Stratagrams which attach to it and challenge yourself to use them more and more.

The real power of the NEXUS Principles is as a set, operating them as part of a whole. Not against each other (on initial reading, they may seem to cut across each other, even contradict in places!), but interacting and knowing which is the primary principle to specifically employ at each situation. What I really wanted to dissect was a set of learnable guidelines for success. My observations of success (with the caveat that it are different things for different people) revealed certain recurring themes and methods which were present in those people who achieve most in their chosen professions, in their businesses, in their roles as parents, in everything they tackled. So, I wanted to simplify, package and offer them as a set of success tools. And as long as we employ them as a set, we will not fall into the trap of thinking that tacking a few tools and techniques onto the outside will make success inevitable. Because, as in the Boy Scout story in chapter one, that certainly would not work.

Business Treacle – a recipe (for disaster!)

This is the favourite food of the Business Groundhog, and when eaten by perfectly sane individuals, it has been known to transform them into these beasts so called because of their tendency to keep repeating the same day constantly (a la *Groundhog Day*, the film!)

The Business Groundhog is the larger cousin of the pet hamster (displaying the same trait of constantly running on a wheel, getting nowhere fast).

Anyway, here's the recipe

- Take one working week
- add an unhealthy portion of emails
- plus a good measure of phone calls and interruptions
- introduce a good measure of hanging around at coffee machines
- add a bucket of 'interesting articles and memos and reports I really must get round to reading some day'
- a handful of poorly prepared meetings
- the minutes of hundreds of now long-forgotten meetings
- sundry scraps of paper reminding me to return countless phone calls
- forms that I really must get to one day when I get chance
- more paper, shuffled regularly
- memos to rewrite in triplicate
- a twist of inter-departmental/people management problems
- as much activity as possible (note: avoid Productivity at all costs)
- garnish with 'The Myth of Perfection' – a common herb, very addictive, and closely related to the spice 'efficiency' (not to be confused with its more healthy cousin 'Effectiveness')
- pepper with an abundance of stories and excuses
- a good measure of 'urgent' mail every morning
- finally, baste with a covering of Blaming and Complaining.

To serve: Sit in the middle and 'try' to wade through.

This dish is best taken whilst wearing a blindfold, or sitting in a darkened office, so you won't be able to see whether you are getting anywhere.

Some people prefer to wallow, rather than wade.

In order to wallow, add an extra dose of Blaming and Complaining. This creates a consistently more akin to mud than treacle. Great for wallowing.

At the end of each day, make sure you save some to put in your briefcase and take home to share with the rest of your family.

Once you have enjoyed your business treacle, at the end of each week, look back and sign up for another dose of the same next week. Take every day (five or even six per week), forty six weeks per year (some like to take it on holiday as well, just to keep the same emotional diet going) for forty years.

Swimming babies: skills and abilities

One of the main presuppositions which attach to all of the Principles here is an understanding of the difference between *skills* and *abilities*.

You may be familiar with the concept of new-born babies being able to swim. Indeed, a well-known television programme shows the image of a swimming baby as part of its title theme. In that image lies a very powerful message for anyone who wants to achieve more in business. It illustrates the fundamental difference between skills and abilities. You see, abilities are things we are born with. And we all have more ability than we realise. Couple this with the fact that most people do not access as much of their innate ability as they would like and this gives a clue as to why most people under-achieve.

Skills, on the other hand, are techniques we can learn. It is my belief that for the vast majority of people in business, we have more skills than we know what to do with, and that if more focus was placed on accessing our abilities, then more of these skills would be used to their full potential. The access to our abilities is leverage for the skills we learn. Isn't it incredible how, when 'thrown in at the deep end', we often surprise ourselves and others? And isn't it also true that in life we often look at others and think 'How is it that I've got all this knowledge, all these skills, I know all these techniques, and yet he is far more successful than I am – he seems to have an air of ignorant confidence which gets him more business than me!' And to us it seems so unfair. I have heard those very words used by many salespeople and other business people.

In essence, what the NEXUS Principles do is to give you the points of access to your abilities, and the Toolkit of Stratagrams and Levers associated with each is the Skill set which will have the most marked impact in achieving your desired outcomes and results. The principles are the tenets which will free you to throw off your success constraints and flourish. People armed with confidence in their ability to stand up and speak in front of a live audience with enthusiasm and passion will undoubtedly give a better account of themselves than people who are steeped in tools and techniques but not confident in their ability to engage the same audience.

Now, in answer to that assertion, many people argue that knowledge of the tools and techniques will lead to confidence. But consider our swimming baby again. Also consider any child who has ever negotiated another chocolate, or a few extra minutes before bedtime. Often by suggesting, for example, that we should be attending a sales course, we quash our abilities in favour of employing the skills. My dog has never been on a negotiation skills course, but –

In addition, if we have knowledge of the full toolkit and the 'best practice skills and techniques', we often undermine our confidence. 'I'll never remember to do all those things!' And before we start, we are convinced we aren't going to perform well.

So whilst the NEXUS Principles are accompanied by a set of appropriate tools, it's the principles which are the guidelines, and the tools are simply an insight into the principles in action. So don't be constrained by the Levers and Stratagrams. They are there to illustrate the principle and to offer some further guidance as to how and where in your business life that particular principle might be employed. Feel free to develop your own toolkit, based on your own experience of what works as best practice for you. But make it consistent. Create habits. Don't just do it occasionally.

You will notice that most of the Levers and Stratagrams are primarily designed to remove barriers, rather than adding any new skills. Why? Because most people in business have most of the skills and all of the abilities they need. But the barriers to their consistently accessing these skills and abilities prevent them achieving successes. So demolishing these barriers to peak performance are what the principles are about – and what the Levers and Stratagrams are geared towards.

The MARS Formula

In order to effect any change or development the MARS Formula is crucial in making the success permanent.

The MARS Formula is;

M indset
A ction
R esult
S uccess

First, the <u>Success</u> or required outcome is identified.

Then the <u>Result</u> (or series of results) needed to effect that outcome are quantified. From this a set of new or improved <u>Actions</u> can be determined which will lead to the results.

Unfortunately, most people and companies stop there. Their Training and 'Change Management' programmes become an exercise in tacking techniques and new actions onto the outside in the vain hope that enough will stick. However, it is crucial to underpin all of this by developing an improved <u>**M**indset</u> which is consistent with the success. If this is not done, the new actions will not be maintained consistently, the results will not be achieved sufficiently and the success will be at best transient. This is a problem encountered regularly by Trainers and Consultants as well as business owners who consider a new set of actions or want to pursue a new idea only to find that in the space of only a few days, the initial disciplines have waned.

The result of this is that, because the **M** has been ignored as a contributory factor, the programme of change is not **MARS** at all. In fact, the worst mistake is recognising that 'something is missing and our people aren't fired up about this yet', to simply bring on the services of a self-styled 'motivational guru' who tacks some Enthusiasm on to the end of the archetypal Sales Conference, creating a whole different mnemonic.

The fundamental element to creating a set of new habits (bearing in mind that people always default to habits) is Mindset. The right mindset will help develop the momentum needed to convert the disciplines (new actions) into habits. The changes begin in the mind before becoming a regular set of behaviours which develop into the default actions – that is, they become second nature.

Initially this will require implanting a new mindset by a process of 'reprogramming' – more of which later. But before we get into that, simply remember the MARS formula.

5

The First Principle – Inner Vision

> **The first of our nine planets: VENUS**
> **Roman God of love**
>
> **This is the principle of Self Love**
>
> **In Holst's *Planet Suite*, Venus is labelled as 'The Bringer of Peace'. And so, true success begins with inner peace and self value.**

The images we hold in our heads about ourselves, our personal positioning in the world, our beliefs, our values have a huge impact on our achievements. They have an impact on our own behaviours, on the behaviours of others towards us, and on the relationships we build with the people around us.

Our outer world is a reflection of our inner world. What we have on the outside mirrors what is going on inside. Because our success in anything is first created within.

Those people who achieve great success invariably hold themselves in very high esteem. They have a very strong and positive inner vision. Outsiders observing them may misinterpret this as arrogance or conceit. But those who are truly successful are simply certain of themselves, they are fully grounded in the life they are leading, and exude an inner strength which is neither conceit or arrogance. It is a sense of unshakeable self-worth.

But, so many people are reluctant to create, or simply not used to creating, positive images about themselves, and often dwell on what isn't right with them.

If your self-esteem is low, it reflects like a wave through the rest of your life. Some of the results can be seen in the world of sport, where an athlete or professional footballer may find their performances dogged by off the field issues. I can think of at least one football player from the modern age who could have achieved greatness beyond that of many others – perhaps been the complete England striker (fast, good in the air, brilliant with both feet, great on the turn, and an instinctive goal-scorer), but who seemingly self-destructed. And so it is in business with so many people who limit themselves because of an inner vision which works against them. Perhaps it's not always evident in such an extreme form. But it is still there. We set ourselves limits which reflect our inner vision, and they are far too limiting. Indeed, we often hold images of ourselves as people who surely 'cannot be successful, because I'm just not like that'.

The ability to build a strong inner vision is therefore paramount.

The SP

Your Starting Point – and your Success Paradigm

Step one is to recognise your own *success paradigm*. A paradigm is simply a model view of the way the world works – and we all have paradigms through which we see the world. We all have a Success Paradigm. This is a belief about what makes up a successful person. Often this will come from our observations of the behaviour of people we admire, our role models. Perhaps it will also be impacted by conversations we had when we were young, along the lines of 'If you work hard and long hours, you too could one day own a car like that, son.' It's not surprising to find many self-confessed workaholics hold onto this paradigm. In essence, our Success Paradigm is our subconscious model of a successful person's traits, behaviours, appearance-style and even thoughts.

If our inner vision doesn't match up with that model, then we are subconsciously telling ourselves that we aren't successful. I know of many people who believe that all successful people get up early in the morning, that all exercise before breakfast, or walk along the beach with the dog, and so on. The result is that if they don't themselves have such habits, they feel somehow to be failing.

Take a few moments to note down all those assumptions, models, and ideas you have which make up your success paradigm – and don't leave anything out. This is most important. Don't think, 'that sounds silly, I'm not putting that down.' If it's there, record it. You can deal with whether or not the idea is valid or logical as a trait of successful people later on. It's important to notice at this stage what your paradigm is.

My Success Paradigm

Once such a paradigm has been identified, the next step is to make up the gap, by behaving in a way which is consistent with the model. But remember that the new actions to make up this gap must be developed into Habits, via the combination of all of the principles, otherwise you will end up with the New Year's Resolution syndrome, of which too many people fall foul!

Subconsciously, many people go through the process of identifying their success paradigm and comparing their current position over the New Year and Christmas holiday period. Perhaps that's why so many people look for a change of jobs just after a holiday period. This personal evaluation generally results in resolutions, or great intentions. But seldom are these maintained, and very few people really keep the intention going for very long. Why? Because they focus on new disciplines rather than developing new habits around their new sense of inner vision.

Of course, very often, we hold things in our success paradigm which, upon examination, aren't true at all. Things like, 'all successful people can survive on less sleep'. Once we have identified these elements of our model, we can remove them, and decide that they have no bearing on our success. Very often, our natural tendency is to feel guilty about not being a certain way or doing certain things to match the model, even when there is no link. So remove the guilt. This is like having a 'Would-Pecker' in our mind, pecking away at our inner vision – 'WOULD-Pecker' because it keeps saying 'you would be successful if you would just do this, be like that, or think like the other.' Or you should/shouldn't do this, that, or the other. Remove the 'Would-Pecker'. Don't let it keep chipping away at your belief in yourself, in your inner self-worth, esteem, value.

The Personal Performance Positioning Perspective

> *'The fault, dear Brutus, lies not in our Stars*
> *But in Ourselves, that we are underlings.'*
> Shakespeare – from *Julius Caesar*

What we believe about ourselves and our capabilities has the greatest effect on our performance and our achievements. It is also a perception of ourselves, not developed in a void, but in relation to our position in the world – our world, and in relation to others around us.

Consider this example and you will see how this affects our performance. You may know of similar examples yourself.

Imagine a sales person, within a sales branch, who has commission earnings of £50,000. This puts him at the top end of the second quartile in Branch One.

Branch One	**Branch Two**
Top quartile (50,000+)	Top quartile (80,000+)
Second quartile (30,000-50,000)	Second quartile (45,000-80,000)
Third quartile (20,000-30,000)	Third quartile (30,000-45,000)
Fourth quartile (15,000-20,000)	Fourth quartile (18,000-30,000)

He is then moved into Sales Branch Two. But the range of performance is different in this new environment. Now, to be at the top end of the second quartile, he would need to be earning £80,000 of commission income.

Guess what happens – Yes. He moves very quickly (within a matter of a few weeks very often) and easily into that position, without consciously changing anything about his performance. His commission earnings rise from the £50,000 level to the £80,000 level. What has happened? He's moved naturally into his perceived position in life.

And beware. The opposite will happen, where the move is in the other direction.

It's our Inner Vision at work.

It's us naturally tending towards where our paradigm of ourselves puts us.

Once we know this effect, we can, of course work on building our inner vision until we match the paradigm. We need to think of ourselves, see ourselves, and actually act the part of the model we want – more of which in the Second Principle.

Professional Modelling

But first, consider the people you do admire. They might be people who have had a significant influence in your past, but you've never really thought about why it is that they appeared so 'together' in some way or other. They may be people who you admire from afar – celebrities, famous and successful people from all walks of life, for example. Or other business people you have observed, whether in your own company, or as business contacts and acquaintances. You can include people from all aspects of your life here. You have a strong connection or admiration for them for some reason. You may not have pinpointed it before, but it's there. So now time to record it and be aware of it. And then to model it.

You can also observe those people who you think aren't quite up to the mark. Whilst I would never advocate being judgemental, it's always interesting to front up why you think someone else isn't up to being a success. You may learn plenty about your own behaviours and habits in doing this! And that way you will be able to clearly see those areas where you really do need to make improvements yourself.

Professional Modelling

Be like	Why?	Not like	Why?

Time to break the chains

A colleague once told me of the one clearly identifiable moment when he was able to make the decision to be successful. Yes, it's a decision. He remembered the moment exactly when he had thought to himself, 'Right, that's it. From now on I'm changing.' It happened when his company, a life assurance company, held a conference. The whole of the sales force was invited, and although this person was highly capable, he felt he was not doing himself full justice at that time. He said that he felt almost ashamed to be there. But what struck him most, was that as well as feeling like a 'nobody', he also felt that others saw him as a 'nobody' too! Whether or not they were in fact thinking that, no one will ever know, of course. But he made a vow there and then. Never again would he think of himself as a 'nobody', and nor would he give any cause to think that others might think of him that way either. He made a promise to himself to become someone. To get recognised and to be a success. Needless to say, he went on to become one of the top two percent of consultants, not only with that company, but within the whole industry, and maintained that top performance consistently throughout his career.

So, decide to *break your chains*. Decide to break out of the constraints which are currently holding you back. Identify your main barriers. And imagine you are literally chained to this huge block of cement. Then close your eyes, and feel the chains releasing and clinking to the ground as you leave them behind. The weight is off. The chains are no longer there to hold you back. You are free at last to move forward.

Successful people hold strong personal images about their own value to the world and their own faith in their abilities. This is their Inner Vision.

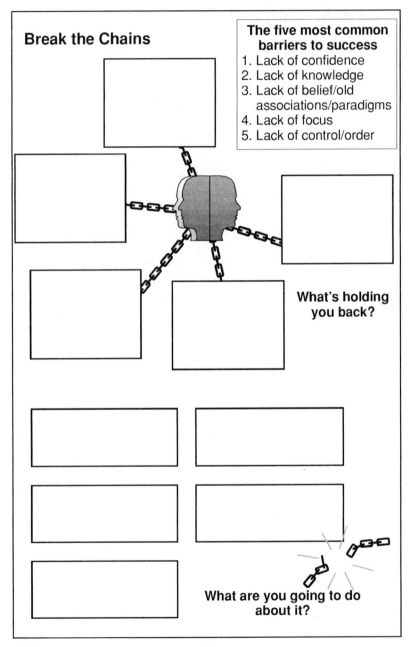

Break the Chains

The five most common barriers to success
1. Lack of confidence
2. Lack of knowledge
3. Lack of belief/old associations/paradigms
4. Lack of focus
5. Lack of control/order

What's holding you back?

What are you going to do about it?

A line in the Sand

ONSIDE	**OFFSIDE**
(what supports me?)	**(what hampers me?)**
Things I currently do, say and think which clearly support me	Things I currently do, say and think which clearly hold me back or damage my inner vision

This is what I stand for, from now on

This is OFFSIDE from now on

Time to Download:

Remember – this is not a chance just to write down things that have been confirmed, but more importantly new things that have been learned.

If you have been reminded of something that you knew but had never done anything about, it can be classed as newly learned. 'To know and not to do, is not to know.'

Action Zone

What I have learned so far ...

What I am going to do about it/use from now on ...

6

The Second Principle – Future Now

This is the Principle of taking massive action immediately, starting with thinking in a new way.

In order to be successful, we need to invent the future for the current moment, by creating the final picture and working backwards. That's how you start to act out the success before it's happened.

Tom Watson of IBM said, 'if you want to be the greatest company in the world, you've got to *act* like it today'. In the same way, in order to be enthusiastic, the best place to start is by acting enthusiastic. You will find that the act creates the reality.

You need to be playing out what you want to achieve in order to guarantee its arrival. And this begins by making your behaviours match your goals NOW. I call this 'Future Now'. It's like fast forwarding into the role you want to be playing, the person you want to be, the business you want to be. Deciding to do this is also very rejuvenating, as it often involves letting go of what is currently dragging you back, and freeing yourself up to behave in a new way – a way consistent with the goals you have.

So how is this principle applied?

Well, start by asking,   'Does my behaviour match my goals?'
then,   'Does my appearance match my goals?'
and,   'Does my attitude match my goals?'

These three questions will help to identify the areas where most work is needed to make a breakthrough. But it's often small things which are easy to change which signal the upgrading to the new you.

For example, I know of a Financial Adviser who wanted to significantly develop his practice by moving into the realms of offering strategic financial and business planning to SMEs (Small-to Medium-sized Enterprises). Step one was to look at his overall professional foundations and change the small things, such as his watch, the pen he was using, the briefcase he was carrying, the diary system and so on. As well as creating a whole new appearance, these minor changes all added up to him thinking of himself and his positioning with his potential clients in a new and exciting way. This subliminal communication is vital for success.

In terms of massively 'ramping up' a company's performance, the same applies. Sometimes it's the small things which, when impacted in a way consistent with the goals, have the company creating new results. This whole principle is about being able to clearly visualise the required and desired outcome, and then fast track to it by acting as if you are there already. Once the level of thinking and the actions are at this new high peak, the results will surely follow.

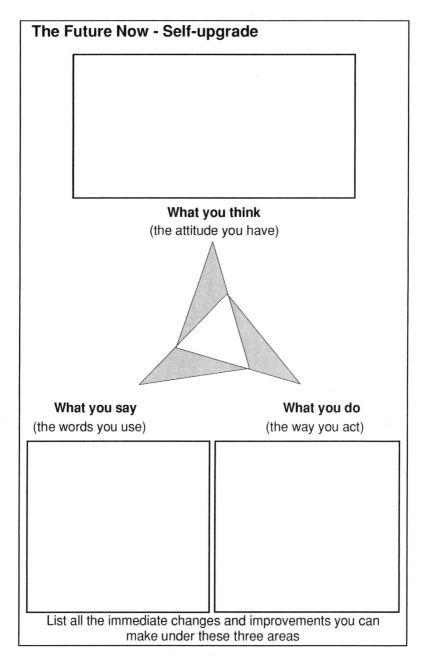

The Future Now - Self-upgrade

What you think
(the attitude you have)

What you say
(the words you use)

What you do
(the way you act)

List all the immediate changes and improvements you can
make under these three areas

Which Division?

It is valuable to view your own performance and that of your business in terms of a footballing analogy.

Professional football in England and Scotland have four divisions each. Premiership (Premier League in Scotland), First Division, Second Division, and Third Division.

If you were to equate it to a football team, which division would you say your business is in? Go with the first answer which pops into your head here, because the gut-feeling response tells us a lot about what you really think of your performance.

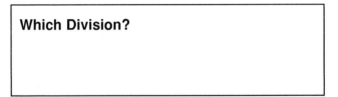

Which Division?

In my experience of asking this question of hundreds of individuals and businesses during coaching sessions, I know that around 80 percent of you will have equated your business to a First Division club. A very revealing answer, indeed.

What are the two criteria which determine whether a club is ready to be promoted from the First Division to The Premiership?

Answer:

- firstly, their position in the table – that is the points they have won
- secondly, whether they have the required stadium and facilities (all-seats and so on).

In business terms we can equate these to:

- firstly, the business results we are getting
- secondly, the environment and structure of our business.

So if we want to upgrade our business to a Premiership Club, we need to look in these two areas, and often we will find some small but significant changes which can be made almost immediately to make us think and act like a top business. Not just good, but World-Class.

And the same is true for our own individual performance.

Those who are successful in any walk of life are constantly pushing up their performance to new heights by asking how they can be world class. And they act on this immediately.

6 – 3 – 1

One of the most important aspects of setting goals is creating balance, as we saw in section one.

This Stratagram creates a tool which allows you to do so, and be constantly fast forwarding on improvements in each area of your life at the same time.

Write the **6 key areas** of your life in the left hand column. These are the six areas which provide the key to your lifeplan and which are the categories for all your goals. These might be Health, Family, Financial, Business – and so on.

Then decide what **3 improvement goals** you have in each area. Write these in the central column. You will now have 18 areas for improvement.

Then decide which 6 things (from the 18) to work on immediately (one for each area of your life).

This Stratagram could be used in a purely business setting by changing the word 'Life' to 'Business' in the first question, so that it becomes 'What are the 6 Key areas of my Business?'

Using this Stratagram on a regular (monthly) basis will create an ongoing continuous improvement ethos and a sense of urgency in generating new strong habits and immediate changes.

6	3	1
What are the six key areas of my life/business	What three things do I want/need to achieve?	Which one am I going to work on immediately?

The Four-piece Jigsaw

This links with the Mountain Stratagram shown earlier, in chapter three. It can be used in any situation where a particular goal is being approached and a 'Base Camp Shopping List' needs to be identified. For example, a career promotion or a business expansion into new markets.

I have found that people often make the mistake in business of assuming that just because they have attended a course on a subject (they have acquired some knowledge) it means they should be moving forward. Many people see extra qualifications as the sole criteria for advancement and promotion.

However, a more balanced approach will create better results, and by looking at Skills, Activity, and Structure as well as Knowledge you will create a long-term solid foundation for business success. In effect, you become advanceable in every aspect, not purely based on technical knowledge. This can overcome the objection to promotion which many people will have heard, 'I know you can do it, but you're just not quite ready yet.' What do bosses mean when they say that? Often they themselves don't know what the missing ingredient is. They couldn't put their finger on it, but they just know a person isn't quite displaying the right signs to be ready to move forward just yet. By constantly 'fast forwarding' across all four areas when you are ready for advancement, it is there for all to see.

Deciding areas for improvement and writing them in each Jigsaw Piece, will give you a more accurate picture of where the priority development needs are. When you have your shopping list laid out, you will find that some elements of it are very easily and quickly fulfilled. You can fast forward to a position of strength once you have seen exactly what you need to acquire in terms of additional knowledge, additional skills, improved activity, and an enhanced support structure.

In terms of structure, it might be as simple as designing your new regime, and some upgraded technology, or even designing your new office layout in detail and then seeing how quickly you could achieve most of the changes. Alternatively, for a business it may mean the restructuring of the workforce, or your immediate team to enable you to move forward. You might need a Personal Assistant, or another marketing assistant, for example.

For activity, a sure way to 'Future Now' in business, is to ask three key questions:

1. If I had a magic wand for my business, what would I wish for, Right Now?
2. If I HAD TO double my business turnover, immediately, what would I do?
3. If I HAD TO double my fees/charges/prices, what would I need to do to improve my product/service which would make it still a good deal for my customers/clients?

The Four-piece Jigsaw

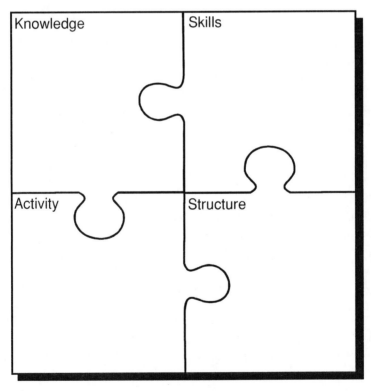

Mirror – Signal – Manoeuvre

This is a very quick-to-use Stratagram which you can employ when you need a bit of a kick, or when you are at a low ebb, and again will help you to identify areas where you need to 'fast forward'.

Based around Learning to Drive, answering the three questions will help to clarify overall strategic direction and generate immediate actions to take. By taking some simple steps you will instantly feel in control and the future will seem brighter. You are also Signalling to yourself that you are getting back on track. This is a strong message to your subconscious which will give you access to extra personal strength.

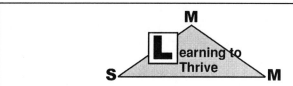

1. Look in the mirror
   What do I see? Where am I heading?

2. What does that signal?

3. What manoeuvres do I need to make in order to change direction immediately?

The Customer Service Gauge

First, plot where you are on the thermometer in terms of customer service. Go with your gut-feeling for this, and then give an example of why you think that's an accurate measurement.

Then, give a full description of what AWESOME/Red Hot customer service would be.

Finally, ask 'What can we do to move to that Red Hot position, IMMEDIATELY?'

Then Fast forward to that role. Act the part. And put in place any quick changes which would exemplify this new Red Hot approach.

Example: Why do I always get offered tea or coffee on arrival at a meeting? Can you do something different for your clients? What about having a very stylish menu to choose from. This will differentiate you from the start. First impressions, and all that ...

Customer Service Gauge

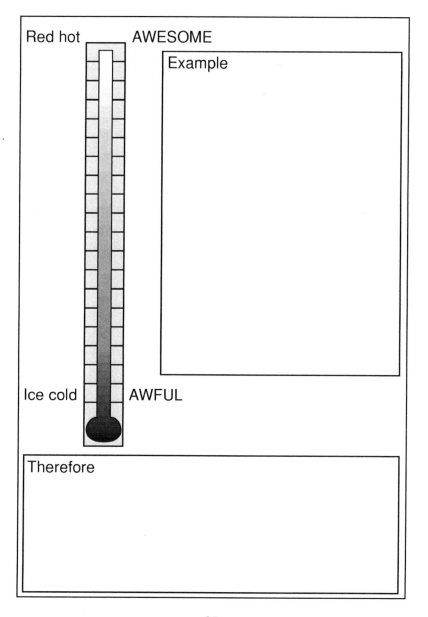

Time to Download:

Remember – this is not a chance just to write down things that have been confirmed, but more importantly new things that have been learned.

If you have been reminded of something that you knew but had never done anything about, it can be classed as newly learned. 'To know and not to do, is not to know.'

Action Zone

What I have learned so far …

What I am going to do about it/use from now on …

7

The Third Principle – Master Plan

> **The third of our nine planets: MARS**
>
> **God of war**

Like a war, this principle is all about the ability to build a strategy to take you from where you are to where you want to be. It's also about remaining strategic on a year-by-year, month-by-month, week-by-week, day-by-day basis. It is about being able to see each activity as part of a strategic overview.

Successful people have an aptitude for planning and remaining constantly strategic – working ON rather than IN their business and their lives. All top performers are able to do that. They can see the whole picture very quickly and cut to the core of any issue very quickly. They have an exceptional knack of getting to the nub of any opportunity or threat because of their overriding focus on the long term. They see individual battles as part of a campaign. And campaigns as part of an even greater plan – just as a guerrilla fighter only fights in the context of a campaign, not simply to win an individual battle.

This principle is all about being able to create a detailed plan of the most effective route to the 'winning post' in a format that really excites you, and which is compelling, where every part of every day has meaning as part of your overall design. It's what I call being able to 'plot your escape route' from where you are now to where you want to get to. All of us need a blueprint that allows us to travel forwards. This blueprint doesn't need to be pages long (it might only be a single page), indeed this is where you can really excel with tools such as mindmaps, and stratagrams.

Using this principle, you can plan in detail the route you are taking to the Vision you set for your business, for your life. It's a written plan, in detail. It will include your Prime Vision, and the 'How', the Strategic Objective. It will also include the strategic steps, the waypoints, the short-, medium- and long-term targets.

It gives you a plan to work to.

You may be familiar with the concept of the difference between working ON your business and working IN your business.

I call this The IN/ON enigma.

- Working 'ON' your business/career/life/finances is about doing the strategic things.
- Working 'IN' is doing the day-to-day.

And the enigma is that most people are running a business which does the technical things which they have the skills to do. So a joiner sets up a joinery firm, a solicitor sets up a legal firm, and a hairdresser sets up a hairdressing salon. Great. But the danger is that in defaulting to habit, the owners spend all their time IN the business, doing the things which they know so well, but spending scant resources or focus ON building the business. Indeed, many find that the only strategic work is doing the accounts on a Sunday evening in a spare time slot!

If you are growing or building a business, where should your focus be? IN or ON? Yes, of course, ON. But how many people truly spend enough of their time and energy working ON?

This concept is explained in greater detail by Michael Gerber in his book '*The E Myth*' and the set of audios '*The E Myth Seminar*', which are fantastic reading and listening for any business person.

This can extend to any area of your life.

This principle is not about having a plan set in stone. It is about having an outline to work to. A set of actions and a timeline in order to measure progress and to help decide on next steps. It must be flexible so that as external circumstances change, then you too can adapt your plan to take full advantage of opportunities as they present themselves, and so that you can take speedy remedial action to bring you back on track when necessary. But you will only be able to take advantage of this flexibility if you spend regular time reviewing the plan and the next steps, the lessons learned along the way, and the changing circumstances and conditions in which you and your business find yourselves.

The Strategy Spectrum

So how do we put the strategy into perspective with regard to our Prime Vision and the Goals we set in section one?

In every field of business, there will be a Spectrum which represents the overall objective for the growth of the business. For example, you might view the desired end result as a large multinational corporation or empire which you want to build in x years. Or you might say that you want to develop a small practice which allows you to fully employ your own skills and knowledge to a set of specific, high net worth individual clients. These two goals (the extreme ends of the spectrum) will require very different approaches. And many businesses fail to identify where they want to reach on the spectrum, and the result is a hit-or-miss approach to building the business. They soon find themselves overwhelmed by opportunities which they are unable to take full advantage of. They have a scattergun approach to marketing their business, and they never establish a consistent brand for their services.

The two ends of the Spectrum I call *Harley Street* and *Wall Street.* Harley Street represents the sort of business which is based purely on the expertise, skills, knowledge and reputation of the individual. Wall Street is a business which has a larger scope of service, and a larger target market, and may grow into a large corporation.

The key to building a strategy which fits with your Prime Vision, is to decide where on the line or spectrum you want to end up.

Similarly, you can revisit this when you reach a crossroads or a plateau to decide where you want to get to, where you are now, and how you can move to redress the balance.

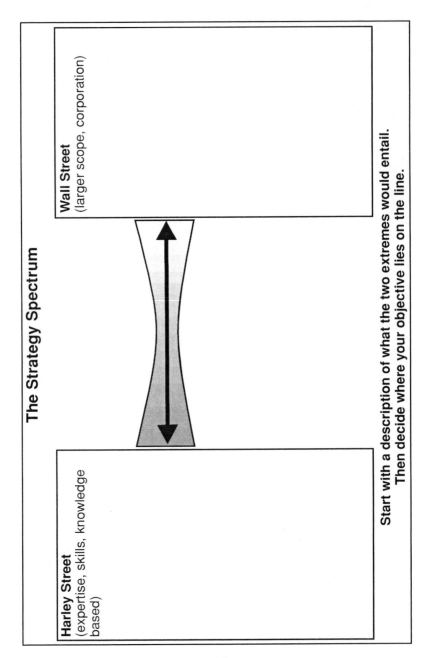

The Strategy Spectrum

Harley Street
(expertise, skills, knowledge based)

Wall Street
(larger scope, corporation)

Start with a description of what the two extremes would entail.
Then decide where your objective lies on the line.

Thinking time

But Master Planning is not just about writing plans. It's about maintaining the space to be able to think. Most people in business appear to be too busy to think! How much thinking time do you have in your week? I'm not talking about idle dreaming time. I'm talking about strategic, productive thinking and decision time.

So resolve to book in thinking time on a regular basis – I would recommend two slots per week, each of at least one hour.

☑ Always think with a pen in your hand.

☑ Have a different chair (or even different room) to think in.

☑ Protect the time. Absolutely no interruptions. This is a meeting with yourself – your most important client.

☑ Balance freeform creative thinking with specific topic thinking. One is about creating new opportunities and projects, the other is about moving existing issues to the next stage.

☑ Use deliberate thinking tools, e.g. Mindmapping, Edward de Bono's thinking caps, or the many Stratagrams in this book.

☑ Understand the limits of your own thinking style and find ways of developing those areas which you haven't used for a while – for example, creative or intuitive.

Your TV panel

Many people find it difficult to think clearly even if they have set aside the time to do so. And often our thinking is clouded by distractions and perceptions of what has happened immediately around us that day. The result is that we sometimes cannot make clear decisions or think through the issues and opportunities which we face.

In order to overcome this 'Inspiration Freeze', set up an imaginary panel of people who you respect and who are inspiring to you. They may be famous personalities, sports people, business people you admire, anyone. Imagine they are on a TV show, hosted by a chair person who is putting to them your set of circumstances.

Imagine the advice they would give you on the way forward, or the way in which a particular challenge can be resolved. The chances are that they will come up with many ideas which you would not have come up with if you had not taken this objective approach. The advantage is that when you choose your panel members, you do so with a certain admiration for their qualities and achievements. You therefore will respect the advice of this panel, and will be certain of it because there is a tacit reasoning behind it from your own gut feeling viewpoint. The panel should consist of between 3 and 7 people.

Coupling this technique with the next idea (Edward de Bono's Thinking Caps) is a very powerful method of thinking through any problem, challenge or opportunity.

Thinking Caps

Edward de Bono has done much in terms of pioneering research into the way we think. As well as being well known for his work on lateral thinking, his ideas on styles of thinking are well worth reading up on. For the moment, I will take a brief look at one of his specific tools: **Thinking caps.**

For most business people, the difficulty is in seeing the whole picture before taking a decision and action on a particular opportunity or challenge. De Bono suggests that many people think only in Black and White when we need to think in full colour to fully identify a range of solutions and thereby pick the best option in any given situation.

He likens the different styles of thinking to separate colours:

White –   Facts, Figures, Data
Black –   Judgement, fitting the facts

Red – Intuition, Gut-feeling, Emotions
Green – Creative
Yellow – Benefits and Advantages
Blue – Process thinking, control of thinking

In order to see the full picture, like a TV screen picture, we must see all the colours.

And each thinking style is like a muscle – the less we use it, the more likely that it will wither and atrophy. The more we use it, the stronger it gets.

So, thinking at a strategic level requires the use of all these styles. Therefore, if we imagine we are putting on a different coloured cap to represent the style we want to adopt, we can deliberately think about each option in full technicolour, even adopting thinking styles which are not our natural bent.

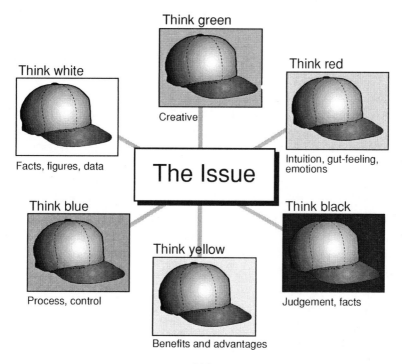

Think green
Creative

Think white
Facts, figures, data

Think red
Intuition, gut-feeling, emotions

The Issue

Think blue
Process, control

Think yellow
Benefits and advantages

Think black
Judgement, facts

Hotel Days

Creating the Blueprint for your life and your business requires **time, focus,** and **energy** in the first instance, and ongoing maintenance using all of those three key resources (more of which shortly).

This is how to do it.

From Alice in Wonderland:

Alice:	Would you tell me, which way I ought to go from here?
Cheshire Cat:	That depends a good deal on where you want to get to.
Alice:	I don't much care where ...
Cheshire Cat:	Then it doesn't matter which way you go

One of my clients echoed the thoughts of so many business people when he told me that the main barrier to creating a clear business direction is lack of time.

When I suggested that we needed a 'Hotel Day', his eyes lit up - 'What's a Hotel Day?'

Well, it's the opportunity to get away from the business environment to put together a strategic blueprint for the future of your business. Armed with a pad of plain paper to capture your thinking, you take a day out – preferably in luxurious surroundings, relaxed and with no interruptions.

For those businesses and business people who do have a clear business vision, the effect on their operations, their marketing, their clients and their own teams stands out a mile. They are more focused, they find it easier to make decisions, they add more value for their clients, and they can transmit a compelling vision to their teams. They also find time to plan the next steps in detail.

'Hotel Days' are now a regular feature in my client's calendar.

The frequency with which you hold these will vary for each individual. However they must be regular – every three months, or every month, depending on your personal style and needs. Every six months seems too far apart for me, and for most others.

If a Hotel Day isn't your style, here's a similar alternative: book yourself a first class return train ticket to take you on a journey lasting approximately four hours. Set aside the whole day. When you reach your destination, simply return on the next available train. One of my clients did this, using the Edinburgh to London service and spent a highly successful and productive eight hours planning, with no interruptions. He called it his 'training day' – training his strategic skills and planning his next steps.

Rules for Successful 'Hotel Days'

1. Block the day off in your diary in advance
2. Create an agenda which moves from macro to micro – life goals to next months targets.
3. Choose a venue with massive associations with quality (e.g. a top hotel).
4. Stick to your timings.
5. Enjoy the day, and view it as a reward for your hard work so far, as well as a strengthening for the next steps.
6. Be clear of all business clutter in advance. Don't let yourself be tempted back to the office to clear up 'urgent' tasks.
7. Create a 'Suspension Bridge' effect throughout your diary planner, with the Hotel Days as supports – spaced frequently and regularly enough to ensure your focus doesn't go slack throughout the year (for some people monthly is too often, so go for quarterly).
8. Cascade the outcomes of the day to your Team within 24 hours (include 'family' as your personal support team). This keeps them focused on the Vision, Mission and monthly activity targets.

Hotel Day Agenda

Here is a sample agenda for your Hotel Day. Of course, you'll find your own running order – but remember to be future-based (this is not a chance to look back at what you have and haven't achieved so far). Also, let the agenda lead you from macro to micro, general to specific.

- ❏ Review Life Plan Mindmap and Prime Vision
- ❏ Blueprint for Business – brainstorm for immediate upgrading
- ❏ Personal Upgrade – 6 -3-1
- ❏ Review Business Strategy Folder (Values, Vision, Mission, Strategy)
- ❏ Review Goals for next 12-15 months (personal, business, financial)
- ❏ Review Mindchangers
- ❏ 'ON' work for next quarter (projects and time slots).
- ❏ Business Source map for coming month
- ❏ Opportunities brainstorm – (special missions)
- ❏ Marketing Engine for coming Month (and time slot regular activity)
- ❏ Prepare **Stratagrams**
- ❏ Strategic Team Briefing

Monthly Planning Days

If a week is a long time in politics, then a month is certainly a long time in business. So, regardless of how frequently you are having your Hotel Days, you need to have some form of strategic planning session every month. These Monthly Planning Days are simply points of punctuation for measuring progress and setting immediate next steps and targets, revisiting short term projects and goals, and following up on opportunities which have presented themselves in the preceding few weeks. Of course, we want to be doing this at all times anyway, but setting aside some specific time on a specific day each month forces us to adopt this as a strong habit.

The final Friday of every month seems right for this and the time you need to allocate will vary from business to business, individual to individual.

Typically, you will need to include:

- Recording of the months results
- Measurement of results versus target
- Setting of next months targets
- Opportunities to work on
- New 'ON' projects for the coming month.
- Improvements to make (in terms of systems, and internal work practices)
- Financial controls and accounts
  ... and so on.

Many people in professional service businesses also include in this session some specific study and research time, especially if moving into new areas of activity and new markets.

WARNING: Be careful not to let the Monthly Planning Day become a catching up on administration day!

The ON hour – ON the Hour!

'There are those who Work all day.
And there are those who Dream all day.
And there are those who spend an hour dreaming
Before setting to work to fulfil those dreams.
Go into the third category,
because there is practically no competition.'
Stephen Ross, Founder of Time Warner

Planning is not just about the long term. It's a daily function, and practising it daily helps you to hone the Master Planning skills.

Spending an hour planning the day's activity can make a huge difference. We will cover more on this in the Sixth Principle.

But this is not just about planning the day. Having a one-hour session working ON rather than IN can move long-term projects far forward rather than having them seen as a huge task to be fitted in one day (or week!) when there are fewer immediate deadlines. Such a time will rarely present itself, so the ability to work the long-term strategy in bite-sized chunks, every day, for one hour, can be the difference between making real progress and simply operating on the hamster's wheel.

Set aside an ON Hour, daily. Protect that time from interruptions, and see how much strategic work you can get done. You will be amazed at the results.

Suspension Bridge planning

In effect, all these specific time slots set aside for planning and strategic work will act like a suspension bridge throughout your business calendar.

This will create a business strategic 'tautness' to ensure you maintain focus. Of course, you must not spend so much time planning that you never act on the plan. But it is essential that you spend enough time planning to ensure the work you are doing fits with the plan, and is therefore productive.

Like a suspension bridge, the planning pillars need to be far enough apart, but close enough together to maintain the right tautness.

Example:

❑ **Hotel Day**: quarterly (or monthly)
    (first Monday of the quarter/ month)
❑ **Monthly Planning Day**: monthly
    (final Friday of the month)
❑ **Weekly Self Organisation Session** (see Principle Six)
❑ **Daily ON Hour**

You will be able to see this suspension bridge effect clearly if you use a colour coding on your planning wallchart. I have always used red to denote strategic planning sessions, with different shape sticky labels for different sessions. Hotel days are a large star, Monthly Planning Days are an inverted triangle, and Weekly Organisation sessions (see Sixth Principle) are a small red circle.

Resource Triangle

Your planning, as with all the principles, requires the adoption of your resource triangle to ensure optimum effect.

Indeed, when you are embarking on any new ASM (Awesome Special Mission) or opportunity, this approach ensures optimum focus to achieve the desired outcome:

We all have these three resources:

Time

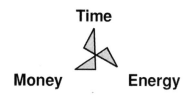

Money   **Energy**

It's no good having two out of three. You must be prepared to give all of these to the activity. Indeed, these three are the foundations for achieving many commitments, and the Resource Triangle is a great tool for deciding on whether to take on a commitment. Ask yourself, are you prepared to allocate all three of these to a project before you embark on it. Similarly, if you are running a business, or responsible for a team, ask whether the project is the best way of allocating these three resources. You should also quantify the allocation as specifically as possible.

This is all about how you leverage your resources to ensure optimum effectiveness. All successful people have the ability to apply these three resources. That is because they apply all three. Not two out of three. It's definitely not a case of '2 out of 3 ain't bad.' Because where our resources are concerned, two out of three is bad. Why? Well, if you apply only two, you probably will not achieve the desired result, which means that you have wasted the two resources you did apply! So it's 3 out of 3, or 0 out of 3 – in which case don't take on the ASM at all.

It is interesting to note that most people in life spend all (or in many cases, more than all) of the money they have each month. In fact, this is true of around 87 percent of people. Ten percent save some money on short-term deposit. Only three percent actually invest actively. Recognise the proportions?

So is it the same with the other resources?

If so ...

! 87 percent 'spend' their time, and expand their energy
! 10 percent 'save' their time and energy, by not risking their full use!
! 3 percent 'invest' their time and energy in everything they do.

I'm looking forward to hearing someone say one day, 'I am retiring to invest more time with my family.'

Apply your resources and view it as Investing in order to achieve the maximum effect when embarking on your ASMs.

Moving Opportunities to Action

OGSM

Stands for – Opportunity, Goal, Strategy, Measurement. This is an often-used management tool, and I have taken it a little further (some say a little too far!)

If, like me, you are constantly looking for opportunities to improve, develop and grow your business, you will have a huge bank of ideas which you store up looking for the right moment. But many of people find that the opportunities never see the light of day, let alone come to fruition.

Put simply, this Stratagram is the way to process your opportunities list to ensure you do something with them. Firstly, use a dictaphone to note down all the opportunities you think you want to pursue. How many times do we think of great ideas when we are in the car, or at an airport, or waiting to start a meeting. You should ideally have around 4 to 6 Opportunities to be working on (however large or small). Adopt this Stratagram for each opportunity. With each opportunity you must identify the Goal. This must be specific and measurable. Make sure it is quantifiable. The chances are that if you can't assign a goal in this way, the 'opportunity' is not ready to go on your list yet. Then identify the series of actions to take you there. The Strategy. Now, this can be a series of small steps (and might include perhaps only a few actions). These actions are a route map to ensure you reach the desired outcome.

Finally Measurement. Decide how you are going to measure:

a) your progress vis a vis timescale
b) the success of the strategy at key points along the way, i.e. the results you need to be achieving at each stage.

To this model I have added an R and an A, not only to make sure I get a laugh when presenting this at a conference or seminar, but also to make the whole idea of working on opportunities a lot more engaging.

The 'R' stands for Reason. And this comes between the 'O' and the 'G', because after we have identified an opportunity, we want to clarify why we see it as an opportunity and why we would want to achieve it, before assigning a specific target or goal to it.

'A' is for affirmation and is the positive statement of how the completed project will look and how we will feel to have achieved it.

These two elements both strengthen the opportunity, making it far more compelling and clarifying the opportunity in terms of the Master plan, the Strategic objective, and the Prime Vision.

When you have achieved one outcome, add another opportunity. It's a great way of making sure you are working on the KEY areas of your business. After all, homing in and focusing on your opportunities is the key to success.

ORGASM Stratagram

Opportunity

Reason

Goal

Affirmation

Strategy
-
-
-
-
-
-
-
-
-

Measurement

Target   Achieved

Time to Download:

Remember – this is not a chance just to write down things that have been confirmed, but more importantly new things that have been learned.

If you have been reminded of something that you knew but had never done anything about, it can be classed as newly learned. 'To know and not to do, is not to know.'

Action Zone

What I have learned so far ...

What I am going to do about it/use from now on ...

8

The Fourth Principle – Persistent Progression

> The planet: EARTH
> The practical realities
> to produce the results.
>
> It is not enough to dream ...
>
> 'The effort has to be based on practical
> realities which produce the result.'
> Stephen Covey

One of the fundamental reasons people fail to hit targets, and in the long run fail to succeed is that they are unable to keep on with their progress. The most successful people develop a **Progression** in achieving their results – along a continuum. This is based around taking action in a specific direction that builds towards the target or goal. It's about activity, moving towards a desired outcome.

In this principle we also have to recognise the massive difference between *Activity* and *Productivity*. Indeed, there are three arenas to be spending time, energy, money on with regard to any work or particular project or goal. **Strategy, Productivity and Activity.** These three arenas are represented in the P-A-S Stratagram. But the two key areas to work in are Strategy and Productivity. The Activity should simply support these two. Activity should be clearly identifiable as a step towards productivity or a strategic development. In too many cases, the activity supplants the productivity without anyone noticing – and is self-perpetuating, leading to a feeling of 'I don't seem to be getting anywhere!' And on occasion the Activity takes on a perceived level of importance whereby it is used (knowingly or otherwise) to prevent work being done in areas of direct productivity.

P – A – S

This Stratagram should be used as a visual prompt to ensure you are putting the most energy into the most important aspects of the day.

Production: This is where you are actually working in your Key Result area. Producing the goods.

Activity: This is general activity. The stuff which is not DIRECTLY productive.

Strategy: This is the Thinking, planning, creative, working ON your business time

Percentage Time Spent: At the end of a day or week simply record the rough score here. It doesn't need to be exact. We are simply heightening awareness of where you have spent time.

Performance Score: This is the extent of the energy, enthusiasm and output you achieved in these task areas.

Use a scale of 1-10 PLUS !

Let me explain:

1-10 is a normal scale, where 1 is a really low score where you could hardly 'get off the starting blocks', and 10 is a highly successful output. Give yourself a score higher than 10 only for those exceptional times where you achieve beyond your wildest dreams – those times when you are at an absolute peak of performance. We hear of how people do amazing things like lifting huge weights off their loved ones in an accident situation. This is beyond the normal range of performance.

This is Peak Performance – a score of 20 !!

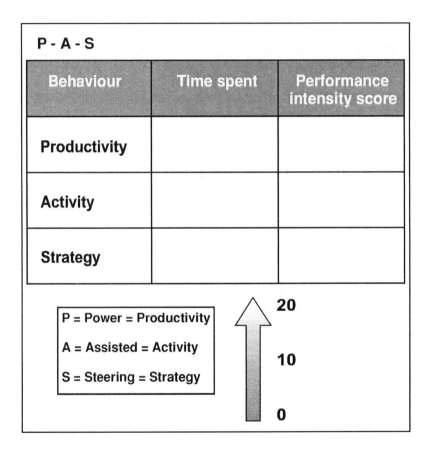

P - A - S		
Behaviour	**Time spent**	**Performance intensity score**
Productivity		
Activity		
Strategy		

P = Power = Productivity

A = Assisted = Activity

S = Steering = Strategy

20

10

0

Productivity is **Power** Output.

Activity must **Assist** the Power and the Strategy

Strategy is the **Steering** to provide direction for your business, your career, your self.

Persistence Progression is about making direct progress towards stated objectives. Being directly productive, and using measured direct action along a track which leads to the achievement of quantifiable results.

This is Progression – *PROGRESS* ion

And when coupled with persistence, this is one of the most clearly identifiable principles which can be associated with the high achievers amongst us. Whether it be business, sport, writing a book(!), learning a language, studying or developing a hobby – whatever it is, anyone will tell you that achievement requires persistence.

Motivation = Motive–Action

Persistence is a function of desire and mental toughness, which are leveraged by Reason. And Reason is clearly linked to focusing on stated objectives WHICH ARE IMPORTANT TO THE INDIVIDUAL. Many companies forget the latter part, and think that simply stating the company objectives or sales targets will provide sufficient reason to do more.

Remember also that there is a huge distinction between Motivation and Mindset. We will be dealing with the power of our Mindset in Principle five.

In terms of motivation, if you have the Vision and the Goals set in the compelling way described in Section One, the motivation will come a lot easier. But so many companies, team leaders and business owners forget that you can seldom motivate others to create lasting changes, enhance performance, or improve results, if you solely apply your own values and goals to the individuals you are leading. It must be their motives which produce their action.

'If you are using a Carrot and a Stick,
Make sure it's a Donkey you are dealing with.'

At an individual level, the reason (or motive) can be a promise of personal reward. Or it can be a threat of denial of a reward. In many instances, the Reason can be self generated, perceived or imagined. For example, the athlete who trains faster, harder and longer, imagining that he must reach the end in a faster time in order to save his family from a terrorist attack. Generating such seemingly unrealistic scenarios and then asking yourself to imagine what would happen if it really was the case – could you do it if life depended on it?!

Investing the Price of Success

With those who are passionate about achieving something, we often stand in awe of their sheer persistence. In fact, they themselves regard it in a different way, not necessarily seeing the persistence as anything more than an acceptance of what needs to be done. They have resolved to pay the price in such a way that it now develops a habit which is painless for them. In fact, they don't see it as 'Paying the Price', but 'Investing the Price'. You don't pay the price for success. You invest the price for success. They just keep on going UNTIL they have achieved the target. They stop for nothing. In fact, the option of stopping does not even enter their head.

Persistent Sting

One of my favourite examples of persistence paying off where others would have taken the easier route, concerns the major breakthrough of the rock band The Police. The band achieved phenomenal success in the late 1970s and throughout the 1980s. The lead singer, 'Sting' is now one of the world's most famous people.

But, of course, it wasn't always that way.

In an interview, Sting (Gordon Sumner) once told of how they achieved their breakthrough in the United States. They were playing at a small venue in New York State, and only three people turned up to see them! What should they do?

They decided to play and, for those three people, they did a full one hour set, and five encores! Little did they know that one of the 'audience' was a local disc jockey who asked for a tape and then played it incessantly on his show. The rest is history.

One of the difficulties with Persistent Progression is that, once our Vision and our Goals are set up in such a compelling manner, we become easily frustrated and impatient at not getting there immediately! This can lead to frustration, or it can be the driver which keeps us going. More often, however, the frustration will come from not actually moving towards the goals at all. Indeed, in being deflected away from them. So make sure that the Progression is in place to allow your Persistence to pay off.

Sometimes, the activity might result in a very small increment (like losing a few ounces of weight, or building money in a piggy bank or savings account). The small-step nature of this makes the progression seem either 'boring' or 'too insignificant' to many people, and very few keep on going. Either they give up, or they change direction, change the goal, change the Strategic objective. And they spend their whole lives changing the goalposts, because they haven't adopted this principle of Persistent Progression to achieve their next steps as a matter of habit.

Taking action in the desired direction on a regular basis will produce success. But make sure the foundations are right at each stage before moving to the next. That's not to say you have to achieve perfection where you are before moving forward. On the contrary. It does mean that impatience can cause you to rush, and expect hugely noticeable results very early – and when they don't materialise, it is that impatience which causes us to give up.

Success is a journey. And if we define it in that way, and realise that deciding to embark on that route allows us to be successful immediately, we can also enjoy the successful journey along the way.

This principle is also about developing a regime to keep things going. It's about developing habits over disciplines. It's about having a daily 'diet' of activities consistent with the success journey you are on. In other words, you create the regime by deciding which elements make up that success. Then you allocate how much time to give to these activities. Then decide when each day, or the format of each week. Then stick with it. We will refer to this more in Principle Six.

The Ratchet concept

Many people say that they feel as if they are always taking one step forward, two steps back! Is this familiar?

Progression is essentially the rate at which you are moving along a 'Ratchet'. The whole idea is to ensure that as you move forward, you also put a foundation in place to prevent your slipping back. Whether it be a new lesson learned, or a new habit developed, you create this foundation before moving forward. Many people start to advance only to find themselves constantly frustrated by the amount they slip back. And often this back slippage occurs very soon after the advance was made.

So it is essential to view progression as a ratchet. Some ratchets are relatively short, requiring only a few steps to be in place to reach the goal. But some can be much longer.

Successful people have successful habits

And unsuccessful people have unsuccessful habits.

So in order to improve performance, we need to work on building successful habits. In our business lives we always default to habit.

Many people struggle to make lasting improvements because they view it as imposing new disciplines which by their very nature are uncomfortable.

But – A 'Pain in the Arse' or a 'Shot in the Arm' – there really is very little difference.

It's all about how you view it.

Initially, the persistent progression will involve some commitment. A lot of commitment. But that is what separates the successful from the rest. They have embarked upon the journey, they are committed, and they develop the persistent progression in such a way that it no longer seems painful to do what needs to be done.

Change how you see it – view the development of these disciplines as the development of a habit.

The psychologists tell us that it takes 28 days to form a new habit. It may take even longer to rid yourself of an unhelpful habit. So developing new performance excellence will take at least 28 days for the new action and focus to become a habit.

The 28-Day Habit Grid

**'Regrets are a terminal pain -
Discipline is a painful fix -
Habits are a painless cure.'**

The human mind gives up to change in somewhere between 21 and 31 days. And so we tend to form new habits in this sort of timescale. I have found that 28 days to form a new success habit is about right, and suits our purposes perfectly.

The Grid is about monitoring progress and at the same time creating a compelling and challenging reason to go on. Initially it's about using discipline but moving the focus towards habit. After all, the discipline of doing something is less painful than the regret of not having done it. Once the habit is formed the need for discipline no longer exists – and what we initially thought was a difficulty has become easy to maintain.

Again, using the 6 areas of your life, and taking a particular point for improvement, simply tick the boxes each day that you perform the new regime. The aim is to have an unbroken run of ticks in boxes from 1 to 28. But only tick in pencil, because if you miss a day you should rub out all of the ticks for that particular habit and start again at Box 1. Once you get to Day 10 you start to want to continue just so you don't have to start again! And soon, there's no way you will miss a day. Before long that discipline becomes a new habit.

The regime you put in place should only be changed if, after 28 days, things are not working out – and only if you have followed the regime for those 28 days.

Don't draw up a regime, fail to follow it, then say it didn't work!

The 28-day Habit Stratagram

	1	2	3	4	5	6	7
	8	9	10	11	12	13	14
	15	16	17	18	19	20	21
	22	23	24	25	26	27	28

	1	2	3	4	5	6	7
	8	9	10	11	12	13	14
	15	16	17	18	19	20	21
	22	23	24	25	26	27	28

	1	2	3	4	5	6	7
	8	9	10	11	12	13	14
	15	16	17	18	19	20	21
	22	23	24	25	26	27	28

	1	2	3	4	5	6	7
	8	9	10	11	12	13	14
	15	16	17	18	19	20	21
	22	23	24	25	26	27	28

	1	2	3	4	5	6	7
	8	9	10	11	12	13	14
	15	16	17	18	19	20	21
	22	23	24	25	26	27	28

	1	2	3	4	5	6	7
	8	9	10	11	12	13	14
	15	16	17	18	19	20	21
	22	23	24	25	26	27	28

'To know and not to do, is not to know.'

Although we are going to cover Mindset in the next principle, it's important to recognise the value of running a regime in terms of its impact on your subconscious. Once you set up a regime, and know you are following it, the signals you send to yourself are very positive and affirm your targets, goals, strategic objectives, and primary objective. Similarly, not following through on the regime you have set up creates self-sabotage.

'To know and Not to do, is not to Know'. We often know what to do, and many people pride themselves on their knowledge of lots of professional effectiveness tools and techniques. At many a seminar, people will say, 'well, it's all common sense, really'. But is it common practice? Seldom!

So although we may know what should be done, if we aren't consistently doing it, we may as well not have that knowledge!

But it's even worse than that. Because when we carry subconscious guilt about what we know we should be doing, and we know we aren't doing it, we send subliminal messages to ourselves that we are not able to be 'successful'.

Many people in sales know they should be doing more of the directly productive things (such as phone calls, contacting prospective clients and customers, and so on) and when they don't do them, the guilt factor is crippling.

Call reluctance is a major source of small businesses failing also. The business owner knows what must be done, but does not use persistence and progression to do these things.

Are you Producing or Excusing?

All of us are aware when we are not doing the things we should be doing to achieve what we want.

It is interesting to observe how people react when you ask them if they have achieved or performed a certain task. Particularly when they are in your team or you are their coach!

The longer the answer, the less likely that they have done the task! They embark on a long-winded set of stories, collisions with circumstance, and 'valid' reasons why the result has not been achieved, yet. They are excusing. Not producing. Now ask yourself, how many times have you 'Excused' to yourself today?

'Doing what the majority fail to do is putting yourself at the head of success's waiting list'.

The minority who Do, will succeed.

So start doing what the majority fail to do.

Persistence is a muscle

So learn how to apply it in all areas of your life, not just in business. Like any muscle, you use it or lose it. If you use it, it strengthens. If you don't use it, it will wither and die.

The whole principle of Persistent Progression is certainly noticeable with the fabled New Year's resolutions. And we all know how most people fail to even keep going beyond the second week in January!

The First Eleven

The eleven keys to making your resolutions stick:

1. Honour promises you make to yourself by finishing what you start.
2. Harness the power of positive pressure by welcoming challenges.
3. Expect adversity and be ready to transform obstacles into opportunities for self-proof.
4. Focus on progress, not on perfection, in order to build confidence.
5. Identify potential barriers and have handling strategies in advance (particularly in the habit-forming phase).
6. Have short-term targets prominent for you and those who can help you directly. Don't have these available to people who can't help at all. Their one askance disbelieving look will be a subliminal missile to destroy your own belief.

7. Make the decision to change. See the targets as part of the whole. And write down what you have decided to change – and why you have decided to change – use the 4X stratagram framework here.
8. Focus on compelling results. Imagine you have already achieved the new regime and it is a habit – and you are enjoying all of the benefits.
9. Write down the key elements you will stick to for the new regime to work and keep these simple. For example 'In order to achieve ... , I will: follow the exercise schedule EVERY day; maintain the Eating Plan EVERY day; drink the requisite amount of water EVERY day.'
10. Understand the continuum and difference between discipline and habits.
11. Use a 28-day grid to form habits from disciplines.

The Rule of 2

An example of creating a regime of persistent progression can be clearly seen in the case of a Sales professional who I coached. He identified that there were 4 key areas which determined whether he got the results he wanted in his business:

> ➤ finding new potential clients (preferably through personal introduction from his existing highly satisfied clients)
> ➤ arranging to meet new clients
> ➤ meeting new clients
> ➤ following up on the meetings he had.

This appeared to be a very simple description of his work, but it also stripped his productivity down to clearly identifiable areas of action.

When we reviewed his targets, he decided that each week he needed to find 8 new clients through personal introduction. He also needed to have 8 quality meetings. He knew that he would be able to convert at least 50% of the personal introductions he received into fresh meetings for the following week to ten days (in fact it soon emerged that he converted far more over time). He also knew that his existing clients would provide an additional four top quality meetings each week.

He rather liked the idea of working for four days and then doing Strategy, Planning and Administration for the fifth day, plus study and reading. So the maths became obvious. His action targets for each of the four days were:

> ➤ get 2 new personal introductions
> ➤ arrange 2 new meetings
> ➤ prepare for 2 meetings
> ➤ conduct 2 meetings
> ➤ do the post meeting work for 2 meetings.

This became his 'Rule of 2'. And he set up his diary to measure this.

> 2,1
> 2,1
> 2,1
> 2,1
> 2,1

When he achieved one of his targets, he would cross off the appropriate number. For example, on arranging a meeting he would cross off the relevant number 2, indicating that he still had one more to achieve that day. This became a ready results-based reference tool. And it certainly kept him focussed.

In your own business, you will be able to work on a similar basis, as long as you accurately identify the key areas.

Your KRAs

Many people are familiar with the Pareto principle, also known as the 80/20 rule.

Pareto was an Italian mathematician and philosopher who

determined that 80 percent of the world's wealth was owned by 20 percent of the population. When this concept is expanded, we find that 80 percent of the sales production comes from only 20 percent of the sales force in any organisation. And 80 percent of the result in any given situation is achieved through only 20 percent of the effort.

So 20 percent of our resources will produce 80 percent of the result we want. What are the activities we are working on which produce the greatest contribution to our success? What sort of things are in this 20 percent?

These are our **Key Result Areas**. For businesses, these will include marketing, sales, strategy and so on. There are normally somewhere between five and seven clearly identifiable key result areas for any business, and for any individual role. So once you identify what these are, you can focus on improving performance in these areas so that the overall result is improved disproportionately. This is leverage.

Focusing only on, say, five Key Result Areas and pushing all of the other activity to the periphery means you can become genuinely productive. Applying the Persistent Progression principle to these areas will ensure you are building habits in the most effective tasks. Of course we don't ignore the other 80 percent which was producing 20 percent of the result. We may find that we must still do those things, because it's often the small things which make the big difference. So we must either delegate to other people whose time and energy will not be wasted in doing these tasks, or we need to set up systems which enable us to do these things using much less than80 percent of our time and energy. More of this in Principle 6.

With our Key Result Areas, we need to create performance standards which allow us to measure and improve performance. We may have little control over the results, but we do have control over the performance. And by adopting the Persistent Progression principle, we will create the successful habits which will generate successful results.

To illustrate this, time for a maths model:

If we are only getting 20 percent of the performance output we want because we are not improving our Key Result Areas.

20 x 20 x 20 x 20 x 20 = 32,000.

Let's call this an Effectiveness Quotient. Compare this with the optimum:

100 x 100 x 100 x 100 x 100 = 10,000,000,000.

Which means that in the first case we are only working at 0.32% effectiveness! (32,000 out of a possible 10,000,000,000).

So, many people are operating at only 0.32 percent of their true value!

OK, so it's a crude mathematical model, but I hope it illustrates the point about working most effectively in your Key Result Areas.

12 Ways to stop procrastination – 'Wait Watching'!!!

One of the major barriers to being able to work consistently in our Key Result Areas is the age old problem of the amount of time wasted through procrastination. So here are some ways of overcoming this.

1. Take time to get organised (see principle 6). It does take time to get your act together, but pays dividends in the fewer wasted moments later on.
2. Begin the night before. Identify the key result areas in advance, and be ready to hit the ground running.
3. Prioritise.
4. Honour your personal work style. When are you at your most creative? When is the best time for you to be doing the routine tasks? When is the best time for you to study? Etc
5. Cat nap to regain energy – most people hit a low point early in the afternoon.
6. Schedule time by blocks rather than tasks. Allocate a given time slot to a task, and aim to complete to a certain point in that time slot. Then move on to the next task. That way you won't get bogged down.

7. With paperwork, make the first touch the *deciding* one. (Not necessarily the *doing* one!) There are some who advocate only touching paper once, and dealing with it at that moment. But in doing so, you may end up working on low priority tasks inadvertently.

8. Worst First! Many people spend as much time worrying about tasks and rescheduling than actually doing them. Look at the projects you keep on postponing, apply the 80/20 rule, and do the 20 percent which creates the 80 percent result. For example, a report following a meeting seems a big task. But breaking it down to bite size chunks, planning it in outline, and putting the notes in order may take only a small amount of time. The task seems more manageable. All you then need to do is aim to complete sections of the report over a comfortable time-scale. Using the persistent progression principle the task will be completed.

9. Create rewards for yourself.

10. Apply the FEVER formula (see below).

11. Start with a small manageable step – just do something about the task you have been putting off. Once you start, the ball is rolling.

12. Schedule a clean up day, or half day, at regular intervals as a clearing up session for all those extra tasks which have piled up. (see Self Organisation session-Principle 6).

Dealing with your procrastination is a means to helping you make progress in the key areas which will make the biggest difference in your business.

If your Business Treacle is so thick and lumpy, you don't know where to start, set aside a Golden Hour.

The Golden Hour

This is an hour set aside at the same point every day. The rule is that during that hour you must only work on your Key Result Areas. There must be no diversions, no interruptions, no procrastinating. Just absolute focus on your performance goals for that day. Only when the hour is complete are you allowed to think about anything else. No meetings should be booked for this time slot. Make it a regular appointment with your own Persistent Progression. You owe it to yourself.

How to get the best from your Golden Hour:

1. Put it in your diary – the most important meeting of the day.
2. Focus on the end vision. Imagine how you will feel to have completed all of the key tasks, and the fantastic results that will produce for you.
3. Make sure you have plenty of physical energy available for this hour. It's no good booking it in for just after lunch! Take a short but brisk walk before starting, to get the juices flowing!
4. Protect the time. Tell your secretary, PA, colleagues that you are undisturbable for the next hour.
5. Have someone take incoming messages for you. That way you can call them back in priority order. Not only is your Golden Hour extremely effective, but your next hour also!
6. Plan the hour in advance – have the relevant files available, the phone numbers prepared, and everything you need close at hand.
7. Work from a clear desk. Keep the one thing you are working on right in front of you, but nothing else. Don't allow your peripheral vision to be cluttered with other tasks.
8. Stay at your desk. Have all of the work piled up in order on the right hand side (preferably on a separate side table). Take one task at a time. When it's finished, move that file to the left hand side (again a separate table if possible). At the end you will have a pile of completed actions, ready to pass on to the next person, or to pass to your PA/Secretary, or to be filed away. Do this all in one go.
9. Batch all your phone calls together. And know what you are going to say in advance. Have a single sheet on the front of each file with notes indicating the key points you need to discuss, or even a mindmap. That way, if you can't get through to the person, and they call you back later, the notes on the file will quickly remind you what you wanted to call about. And you won't forget one item.
10. Once the Golden Hour is complete, reward yourself. You have

probably completed the equivalent of one full day's work in a single hour. You've certainly done 80 percent!

Awesome Special Missions – creating breakthroughs using the FEVER Formula

As I referred to the FEVER formula above, this is perhaps the best place to explain how the formula works. So here is a very simple formula to help you approach every ASM in a way which ensures you can get best results;

F = Focus
E = Energy
V = Vision
E = Enthusiasm
R = Reason

Focus – beyond the goal/objective. In order to breakthrough a target, you need to be focused beyond it, on what the achievement of the target means to you.

Energy – include some very positive action as early and as urgently as possible to ensure a good start. Physical energy can help with the most basic business functions. Standing up to make an important phone call, for example.

Vision – have a strong mental image of the completed task, in as much detail as possible. Literally see the task done in your mind's eye.

Enthusiasm – we will cover this lots more in Principle 7. Coupled with energy, in any action, this will engender speed. When you have energy and enthusiasm, you can't help but get the job done in optimum time.

Reason – have a strong reason for doing the task. It must be a personal reason – and make you want to peak perform. Offering yourself a reward for successful completion is a strong motive.

At my seminars, I have often illustrated this point by creating a real breakthrough with a participant who gets to break through a wooden board (karate style) using this formula. The Focus is at a point beyond the wood. The key skill is to make the required action with speed (not strength). Energy and Enthusiasm do the trick here. Having a clear image in mind of the board broken in two is crucial. The reason is created by peer group pressure and support, and also by imagining the scenario where the board must be broken through in order to rescue loved ones from a fire. This is immensely powerful, even though the situation is purely imagined, the mind which creates the desire and generates the reason has something tangible to equate the whole exercise to.

Using this formula will help to set up you and your teams for taking full advantage of your opportunities and ASMs.

The Rule of 7

The Marketing Guild's analysis shows that it takes, on average, seven contacts to gain a significant business order. And, on average, most people give up after two to three. Applying this to the 20 percent of clients who are in your target client profile (and who will generate 80 percent of your business), will have a massive impact on the way you view the marketing of your services. Most people run out of ways in which to make contact and after two or three phone calls, they simply stutter to a halt and give up. But we can make the whole thing far more interesting and valuable if we have a number of different modes of contact. This raises awareness and allows you to apply the 7 contact rule more easily. This is persistence without being a pest, and by being creative.

The Marketing Engine

One of the fundamental reasons so many businesses fail is lack of regular marketing activity. The marketing engine is about creating a 'clockwork' system of activity which ensures a steady flow of new clients. The result is that once the Engine is designed, the Persistent Progression Principle can take effect. Very often, with an accurate and well-tuned marketing engine, a small business may need to spend only a small amount of time actually doing the marketing tasks. The engine has been designed to create a result through small manageable components all operating consistently and persistently.

The principle is that many businesses market through only one type of activity. However, the marketing engine should contain a mix of Direct marketing and Indirect marketing – targeted approaches and profile building.

Aim for running at least four cylinders and preferably six, possibly eight. Each cylinder represents a particular strand of marketing activity. The strategy for each cylinder is simply the step-by-step actions which need to take place. Break these down into daily actions. Once the engine is designed, it's amazing how little activity is needed to create great results. The key is that something is happening about proactive marketing every day. And when the engine is generating runaway success, don't turn off the cylinders (as many people are tempted to do – thus creating a Boom/Bust profile). Instead, simply regulate the flow by turning the cylinders down. It's much easier to turn them back up at a later date than it is to restart old dormant cylinders from scratch again.

I have found that many businesses need to draw out a new marketing engine each month with specific activities allocated to each day of the month.

7 steps to building a marketing engine

1. Have a minimum of four cylinders of regular activity operating consistently.

2. Balance the engine between hard marketing (direct approaches) and soft marketing(indirect approaches, PR and profile building).

3. Include a creative edge to each of the cylinders which appeals to your target market.

4. Each cylinder represents a system or pattern of activity – a schedule which you can then diarise. So even a one or two-person business can maintain the engine by doing a little but often. Most businesses leave marketing to chance and end up having to do too much at one go.

5. Each cylinder must be followed through to conclusion. Don't give up half way through the process.

6. Measure and quantify the results.

7. Review the engine at regular intervals as part of your strategic planning, and decide on any improvements and adjustments to be made.

Marketing engine

Idea

Potential

Strategy

Day/date 1

31

Time to Download:

Remember – this is not a chance just to write down things that have been confirmed, but more importantly new things that have been learned.

If you have been reminded of something that you knew but had never done anything about, it can be classed as newly learned. 'To know and not to do, is not to know.'

Action Zone

What I have learned so far ...

What I am going to do about it/use from now on ...

9

The Fifth Principle – Mindsetting

The next of our nine planets: JUPITER

Mindset has the greatest impact on the achievement of our success.

Many successful people find it difficult to put into words what they are doing which makes them successful. They don't see themselves as putting any extra effort in, or summoning up huge reserves of motivation, energy or effort. Indeed, most of them can understand what makes people unsuccessful! They can grasp why most others don't 'just do it.' And that is because they have such a powerful mindset that they are able to just do things others would not consider, or that would require a huge injection of motivation or a drawing on the deepest of reserves. They just get on with it, and consistently act at the peak of performance without thinking about it. They have successful habits, and that's that.

This principle is all about emulating this mindset, and reprogramming our own mindset in order to reach forward to the next level in our own journey to success.

This was going to be the longest chapter, because the use of these tools will have the most powerful impact, and there is so much to be said about the ways in which the techniques work through the application of our subconscious to the task of achieving what we want. However, the scientific background and rationale is not the subject of this book, and nor am I the person best qualified to lead you through psychological and scientific theory here. The research being put into the workings of the human mind is ongoing and never-ending. It is an area of scientific analysis that has seen massive growth and yet, as we explore, we uncover only enough to ask more questions. All I can say is that the tools work. And they work well. And they work quickly.

This chapter was also to be filled with examples of situations where the power of the mind has had an impact on the results of an individual whether in business, sport, politics, or any form of human endeavour. However, as you will have realised by now, these stories are in everything we do and see on a daily basis. So having read so far, you will know by now that all of the Principles in action are underpinned by this fifth principle. No need for page after page of examples – there are many books which cover such ground.

This chapter is therefore, simply an outline of the Mindsetting techniques which I have used extensively myself and with others. And I have found that they really do work!

Interference

We looked at some of the barriers and blockers to success in chapter four. However, the most fundamental barrier to success and achievement for the vast majority of people is something I call **Interference**. It is the psychological barrier between knowing what we should be doing and actually taking action.

Most people know they should be making more sales calls, or spending time getting themselves organised, or plotting the time in their diary to plan, or writing up a report, or seeing more clients, or creating a powerful business vision. But whilst most people know it, very few are able to do it on a consistent basis. Think back to our daily action plans. Most people know they should be doing them, but very few do them.

The barrier exists in between our ears. It's like a virus in our necktop computer system. It either makes us do the wrong things, or it makes doing anything very slow and sluggish. Breaking this interference is critical for making improvements in performance – whether it be sport, business or any field of activity.

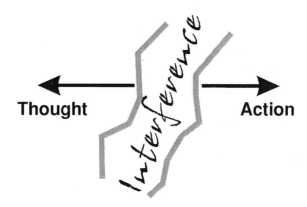

Have you ever been to a seminar or training course, or listened to any tape or read any book on personal and business growth, and found that, even though you were full of ideas to 'try things out', a very short time later the high intentions have slipped, and the enthusiasm waned?

If you have don't worry – you are not alone!

Most people fail to implement even a small percentage of their countless ideas around performance improvement.

Interference leads to FTI.

And FTI (failure to implement) is the key reason people fail to make the desired improvements in any areas of life – whether it is business related, or going on a diet, or an exercise regime – whatever the goal. And it is also the key to why most management training does not produce results consistent with the level of investment, in terms of time, energy, and money. And this is something I have personally worked on for a number of years – implementing a simple and effective individual support structure around all management development programmes, after the event. This focuses on how to underpin the training by working with individuals on their mindset development. Remember the MARS formula?

Most people have great intentions to make performance improvements, but returning to work to an 'In Tray' the size of Istanbul doesn't exactly help. And if the new ideas are not acted upon, they are very quickly forgotten. They will certainly never become a habit. And yes – don't forget, it's habits which will determine our level of success.

The aim of creating a powerful mindset is to allow ourselves to break though the interference.

FTI = Failing to Implement.

No. We want to be fully in tune – FIT.

FIT = Fully in Tune, no Interference.

The source of the interference – Buzz and Fuzz

Fuzz is the sum total of all our self-doubt, personal position paradigms, associations ('I've never been any good at …') and results in our not being focused on the goals and objectives we have. It allows our minds to wander rather than enabling us to concentrate, and it prevents us accessing our true abilities. We hold back – and we don't even know we have held back. It's automatic.

Buzz is what other people give us – it's reflected self-doubt. It's the askance look from our colleagues as we calmly announce at coffee time that 'I'm going to have my best month for sales ever.' They don't even need to say anything – their look says it all. 'Yeh, sure. We've heard that before! Been on one of those motivational seminars have we?!' And we think, 'Yes, I know. I've said it all before haven't I. Well I'm going to do my best for a few days, and then it will all be forgotten until next time!' Result – we don't even believe it, just as the statement leaves our lips.

One of the keys to countering the BUZZ is to avoid telling people any of these things – any of our goals, objectives, targets – unless they can help us achieve them. Don't go around collecting this interference. Only connect with those people who can and will support you – unconditionally. And especially, don't go telling others the mindsetting techniques outlined later in this chapter.

Conscious/subconscious interference – fight fire with fire

All of this interference happens at a subconscious level. And that makes it all the more powerful. Because it's that part of our mind which holds the vast majority of our performance power. The subconscious represents around 95 percent of our mindset. It's the part of the iceberg which is below the waterline. It controls our behaviours at a subliminal level. It will always override the conscious mind.

For example. If you are watching a frightening movie on TV, whilst your conscious mind is saying 'It's just a movie', the subconscious is reacting to the images and making us display all the behaviours associated with being afraid – racing pulse, increased heart rate, sweating palms. So our subconscious controls our behaviours.

In essence, the Human Mind doesn't understand the difference between what is real and what is imagined, as in the instance of the scary movie.

So, if the subconscious controls our behaviours, and the human mind doesn't understand the difference between what is real and what is imagined, then in order to improve performance behaviours, we must create powerful images of ourselves performing brilliantly, get the subconscious to believe them, and then allow the subconscious to enhance our behaviours accordingly. Sounds simple.

So, how do we do it?

Well, in essence, we need to reprogramme our mindset to see different images, expect and believe different performance levels. Then the mind will challenge reality to catch up. It will improve our behaviours so they become consistent with the images we now have in our heads and inevitably the results consistent with these new behaviours will follow. Remembering back to the MARS Formula. The **mindset** will lead to **actions**, which will lead to **results**, which will lead to the **success** we identified at the outset.

Mindset Domes and Comfort Zones

The phrase 'Comfort Zone' is now a household term and a familiar concept to most. In its simplest form it describes that part of our motivational make-up that is between the pain and pleasure of both failure and success. We take the path of least resistance and continue to do the easy and comfortable thing, which neither stretches us to new heights of achievement nor threatens our current security.

Sadly, I believe, it is a commonly unquestioned tenet of most 'skills' trainers and coaches to constantly bark on about getting people to step out of their comfort zones in order to make changes and achieve new successes.

Why do I say 'sadly'?

Well, if we get people to consciously step out of their comfort zone, we are employing a discipline. If this discipline is not backed up by developing a new mindset, the necessary habit will not be formed, and in a short space of time the individual will step back into the comfort zone. This is especially so when the going gets tough. People tend to run for cover when they aren't hitting the new heights they so badly wish for. And worse still, the comfort zone will not only be unchanged in scale, it will also be reinforced by the new sense of guilt/failure that as well as the whole episode being an unpleasant and uncomfortable experience, it was also a fruitless one, or at least the results were very short-lived.

'The mind once expanded can never regain its former shape.'

If we haven't expanded the comfort zone and encouraged the individual to operate at the extreme outer limit, we can't create a lasting change.

A better representation might be to consider our mindset as a dome:

We are positioned at the centre of the dome and all of our self-imposed limitations, beliefs, attitudes, associations and paradigms create an overarching barrier. We can only achieve what is first created in our mind, and so in order to take new actions to improve results on a consistent basis, we need to first expand the mindset dome and then operate at the new 'outer limit'. We must allow ourselves to believe, at a deep subconscious level, that our new performance is not only achievable, but is in fact already being achieved. We must first imagine ourselves operating in the 'stretch zone' which then sends the signal to our mindset that we are achieving new heights. This belief will allow our new set of behaviours to become habits because they don't seem to be uncomfortable actions, as they are consistent with the extent of our newly stretched mindset dome. We find ourselves accommodating new habits much more quickly. The MARS formula is at work.

So rather than getting people to step out of the comfort zone, work on expanding the mindset dome and then challenge the reality to catch up.

All of the Mindsetting techniques rely on this same format.

Mindsetting Technique # 1

A game for partners – Time Travel Talking

This follows the vein of the time travel exercise earlier in the book.

This requires two people to have a conversation set in the future, and to say it as if it was the present. Take around two minutes for this. One person is simply listening and asking a few questions to encourage the other person to add more detail and describe in vivid terms the successful achievements which they have experienced and made happen over the preceding three years.

Setting the conversation around three years on is about right. Imagine you are meeting for the first time three years from now, and catching up on all the news. Imagine a magic wand has been waved and you have had the most unbelievably successful three years and your life and business/ career are all you ever wished for. Include as much detail as possible, with colours, sights, sounds, feelings. Really picture yourselves there. Make it believable and compelling by going with your gut-feeling. Let the description flow. Don't hold back on what you really would love to have happened.

Capture this all on audio tape. And then play it back and write out the detailed vision.

Change over roles, so that you can both have the benefit of the technique.

Review this around once per week initially (for a month). Thereafter, once per month is about right.

Mindsetting Technique # 2

The Cards

Write out all of the things you want to change and achieve in the next 12-15 months. There should be a minimum of 20 items, and not more than 30. They should closely relate to your tactical targets and awesome special missions. In addition to results oriented targets, include personal performance improvement areas, for example improving confidence, or delegation or time effectiveness, or being more influential at meetings of more energetic.

Put each individual aim onto a separate index card – around 6 inches x 4 inches.

These should be from all areas of your life; business, personal, financial, social, family and so on.

Write them as if they have already happened. And include powerful language, especially at the start of each statement.

So...

' I want to lose weight and get down to 11 stone.'

Becomes:

'Wow, it's fantastic how fit and healthy I feel now that I am 10 stone 11. I feel so confident and everyone notices how great I look.'

The use of very powerful superlatives at the start means:

➢ The focus is not on the goal itself, but on what it will mean to achieve the goal. In other words, we are reiterating the reason behind the goal. That is more compelling than the target in itself.

➢ The subconscious attention is grabbed. The powerful words say, 'Hey – listen to this' above all the ambient information and data being absorbed by the subconscious all the time. If you are reserved, and they are not the sort of words you would normally use, so much the better.

Once you have a set of these cards, simply read them at least once a day. Set aside the time to be in a personal, quiet location, and spend ten minutes reading the cards. When you read them, do so word for word. Really see, and feel as if you are there, having achieved the result you are looking for. Don't simply look at the card and think 'that's my losing weight card – good, I know that one – move on.' I have found that the best time to read the cards is first thing in the morning. Don't rush out of the house thinking you can catch up on them once you get to the office. Unless you have your own specific space for this, you will find it too easy to be distracted by the early morning business treacle.

These cards must be read every day. Start off by setting the challenge of doing 28 days unbroken. Saturdays, Sundays, holidays, all included. The key is again, habit. It's about retraining your mind to work in a certain way, to believe new things about yourself and your performance.

Avoid negative language or images of any kind. So instead of saying 'It's great not to feel fat anymore,' we would say 'Wow, it's great to feel really healthy and fit now that I am ...'

This is very important as, in order to think of 'not fat', the mind has to think of 'fat' – i.e.. you create an associated image.

You will need to renew these cards on a regular basis with a view to creating new cards, removing those which are achieved. When you do remove the cards which are achieved, don't discard them. Keep them in a place close to your blank index cards. That way, you will gain extra strength when you are about to write out a new and seemingly very challenging card to add to your pack, as you will see all those previous cards which at one time also seemed so challenging.

Mindsetting Technique # 3

Stargazing

Take a piece of coloured card. It should be 6 x 4 inches and brightly coloured – red, green (or my personal favourite) blue.

Stick a gold star on the card (the sort children use in their school exercise books). Put this just off centre of the card.

This technique uses the power of a strong mental association and creates a trigger to ensure peak performance when you need it most. It's the sort of technique used by sports people when they are about to perform.

Generate a powerful image of the next specific material thing you want to achieve. The thing which is currently just out of reach.

Now picture this as if it has happened and you have acquired the item (it could be a new car, house, client).

Hold the Star card about 16 inches from your eyes, tilted slightly so that the light can reflect off the card. Look at the Star. Now think of the picture being behind the star. It's right there.

Behind the star – in the star.

The picture is specific and detailed. Think of the colours, and include action, with you involved. Yes, you are right in the picture.

Spend approximately two minutes, looking through the star, seeing the picture and imagining it has happened.

The Star acts as a trigger for your mind. Once you have carried out the technique, look at the Star card at intervals during the day – before important meetings, for example. This might only be for a fleeting second. But the picture of the Star will generate an association with improved results in your mind, which will generate an image of enhanced performance. And as your subconscious doesn't differentiate between what is real and what is imagined, it then goes on to modify your behaviours to match what it believes you are.

Carry the card with you.

Also have Gold Stars strategically placed around your office – on the phones, PC, diary, etc. These triggers are now all around you. Indeed, you can put Gold Stars around the home, such as in the bottom corner of your TV screen if you spend too much time watching unplanned TV. The star will remind you to get up and do something more productive.

You become subliminally aware of the star. It is a very simple shape, and the vivid colours (gold star on blue card, for example) are an excellent trigger for your subconscious. The powerful associations remove Interference.

Mindsetting Technique # 4

The Lift

Sit down, close your eyes and relax.

Imagine you are in a lift (elevator). You are on the 20th floor of a building. You start to travel down in the lift.

Countdown from 20, through 19, 18, 17 and so on to the Ground Floor. This takes around 15-20 seconds. As you descend in the lift, relax from head to toe. As the lift descends, relax each part of your body from the top down. The whole idea is to get yourself to such a relaxed state that your mind is empty of distractions and you can give it a powerful image.

You reach the ground floor. The lift doors open.

In front of you is a clock. On it is your favourite time of the day. It does not matter what that time is, as long as it is the same each time you do the technique. For most people it will be somewhere in the morning between 7 and 11am.

Imagine yourself turning to the right. This is a very important part of the whole technique as it helps you to access the right side of your mind, which is the creative part of the brain.

You proceed to the right and find yourself in a room where the epitome of personal success is for you. Imagine it actually happening – giving a public performance, or being rewarded at the company conference. This vision should be close to your Prime Vision, or a major goal for the longer term. But see yourself experiencing it now. Feel the emotion of that moment, hear the sounds of people congratulating you. What are they saying? What are you saying? Hear the applause. Is there music playing? What are you wearing? Imagine how comfortable you feel. Like a million dollars. A massive smile stretches across your face.

Really be in the situation. Allow this to go on for around4 minutes.

Then return to the clock. It now reads one hour on from where it was when you started the exercise.

Return to the lift, and then proceed back to floor 20, 'unrelaxing' as you go. And that's the technique finished.

Many people find it difficult to relax in the first part of this exercise. So, what should you do if you can't relax? Many people find that within only a few seconds of getting in the lift that once they have cleared their immediate thoughts out of the way, they start thinking of other distractions – that important phone call to make – or 'I must remember that letter', etc.

Don't worry. Go through the process of the whole technique. You will gradually, over time, train yourself into the technique – improving the quality each time you do it.

Many people like to use a particular piece of music to help to relax here. Played through headphones, this can act as a further anchor for the image in your mind, particularly if you also play that piece of music at specific other times during the week.

This is a very powerful Mindsetting technique, possibly the most powerful of all the techniques. It should be used daily initially (say, for 2 weeks) and then at least twice weekly thereafter.

Mindsetting Technique # 5

The Train

This is a tool for getting rid of any traits you have which are damaging or which hinder you in any way. For example, you might see yourself as timid or under-confident. Or overweight. Or not good at networking.

Imagine yourself on a train. The train is sitting at a station and on the platform is you. Or more accurately the old you (or you might think of this person as your old 'twin'). And the old you is displaying all of the actions you want to get rid of. He or she is behaving in the way which you think is currently holding you back, displaying all your old traits.

Now the train starts to pull away from the station. You wave goodbye to the old you. You feel the amazing sense of leaving those traits behind forever. The person fades into the distance. It is no longer you.

As the train finally leaves the platform behind, you feel the sense of freshness. You are now the new you – sitting on the train displaying all of the strong traits you want to be associated with the new you.

You feel, hear yourself, and see the impact of the new you. And you feel so relaxed and delighted with the new habits you have. You find it easy to stand tall, puff your chest out and confidently walk into a room full of strangers and network with them, for example. They are all delighted to meet you and want to do business with you, and you are the life and soul of the gathering.

This technique takes about 90 seconds and should be done on a daily basis for best results. Lunchtime is a good time for this as it is quick, easy and offers a burst of energy for the afternoon.

Mindsetting Technique Strategy

Time Travel Exercise - once a week (for one month), then once a month thereafter

Cards - daily – best first thing in the morning

Stargazing - daily, after the cards

Lift - daily for two weeks, then twice a week – after the Star.

Train - daily – good around lunch-time, to recharge energy, or before significant events, e.g. a meeting.

When used on a regular basis these tools will produce amazing results. Find your own personal working style with them. But, do do them. They really do work. As always, the principle needs to be applied. It won't happen by magic. And at first that means doing something about it.

Important Note

This is not about magically conjuring up/voodooing your way to success.

It's about removing interference which means you will take action and perform in a way which is consistent with your goals. Even at a subliminal level, your behaviours will alter which in turn will create different results. You will achieve results which are consistent with your goals. Using these techniques will allow you to take consistent and habitual action to lead you to your goals, without you even thinking consciously about the actions you are taking. You will start going the extra mile, saying the right thing, acting a certain way, improving your posture – all of which add up to improved performance. These little improvements in so many areas will create hugely different results.

> '*Projecting your mind into a successful situation is the most powerful means to achieve goals. If you spend time with pictures of failure in your mind, you will accelerate failure.*'
>
> Estee Lauder

Time to Download:

Remember – this is not a chance just to write down things that have been confirmed, but more importantly new things that have been learned.

If you have been reminded of something that you knew but had never done anything about, it can be classed as newly learned. 'To know and not to do, is not to know.'

Action Zone

What I have learned so far ...

What I am going to do about it/use from now on ...

10

The Sixth Principle – Double O – Order and Organisation

Our next planet: SATURN

The god of time

Making effective use of Time is a fundamental key to success. And successful people are effective with their time because they have the foundations of Order and Organisations in place.

Order and Organisation – what's the difference? Well I'm not one for being picky, or relying on strict definitions. But for our purposes here, I have taken 'order' to refer to the sorting out of things past, and the physical ordering of things present, as a platform to moving forward and to allow the focus to be on the future. 'Organisation' refers to the development of regime, prioritisation and time effectiveness consistent with the future goals, reflecting where we want our business and ourselves to move to. In short, order is about creating space (in terms of physical and psychological space) and organisation is about creating regimes.

A recent news story got me thinking. You may be familiar with the story, and you may know more of the detail than I. However, briefly the story was that a NASA space probe which was orbiting the planet Mars began to experience some technical problems. Conducting a diagnosis via computer, the team on earth were able to fix the problems. But to their surprise within a few minutes the Probe had disappeared from all contact and subsequent investigation revealed that it had spun from its orbit and crashed into the planet. So what had caused this malfunction? Simple. When the orbit co-ordinates had been reprogrammed after the maintenance work was completed, they had been fed into the Probe's computer in imperial measurements (feet and inches), whereas the Probe would only understand metric measurements! When I heard this tale, I was amazed and thought 'How stupid!' I mean, these things cost a few dollars (or pounds, euros, etc). What a costly mistake. But isn't the same true in all business. It's the simple things which make the big difference. The things we pay little attention to are often the things which most cause us to fail in our own missions. And so often this is the case where order and organisation are concerned. The principle of Order and Organisation is about getting the simple things right as a foundation for greatness.

Order, Order!

Order first then. In order to allow our futures to arrive, we must let go of all those things hanging over from the past. This involves a literal spring-cleaning (or business colonic irrigation!) and may even spill over into areas of personal life. How great it feels to have had a huge clear out of all the unneeded files, paperwork, and even a serious clear up of our office space. We can all relate to how good it feels to be working from a clear desk. Remove the clutter and allow the future to arrive. You might like to start by designing your next office (on paper) – the office you would dream of. And then see how close you could get to that in your current office by simply rearranging the space and the work.

A significant advantage from ordering your environment is that it firmly grounds you in the present. You have chance to make decisions to get rid of all the things that are not relevant to The Now. I am certainly not puritanical in insisting on minimalism, nor am I fully conversant with the Feng Shui gurus. However, much of what they say at a very practical level seems to make eminent sense, even if you don't necessarily subscribe to all the attendant universal philosophies! Removing your past baggage certainly helps in the same way that having a spring clean produces a sense of relief and readiness for moving forward. Of course, there will be things you want to keep from the past. But make sure they are of significant value for the present/future. And ask that very question, 'of what value is this NOW, or will it be in the future?'

As well as sorting out the physical clutter, it's important to sort out any other baggage from the past. Whilst many books in the psychology and self help sections of libraries or bookshops can offer detailed guidance here, let me simply offer some practical advice. Simply write down all the things that fall into this category of 'hanging over from the past' and sort them out in priority order (perhaps in several stages using the fourth principle of persistent progression).

There is a significant side effect to all this 'getting sorted out' business. Let me explain by playing a little game – and bear with me. I want you to think of someone famous who you admire as being successful, or perhaps someone who isn't necessarily famous, but who is a successful person in your eyes. Now, when I do this exercise at seminars many people think of someone like Richard Branson, for example. Whoever you have chosen, get a clear picture or idea of them in your mind's eye. Now I want you to picture them in their office. Go with the gut-feeling vision you have of them standing by their desk, or sitting at the desk working. The chances are that the vision you have is of that person in a clear office with very little clutter. Why ? You see, I've no idea whether Richard Branson has a clear office or whether he works in a complete tip! It doesn't matter. What matters is the natural association we have between thinking of a successful person and what their office would be like. In fact, we have a subliminal belief that successful person = clear office. Similarly, the converse is true – cluttered office= unsuccessful! So what message are we carrying as part of our Success Paradigm if we are in a disordered office? Exactly – we are telling ourselves 'cluttered office, therefore I'm not ready to be successful yet'. Certainly this association supports what many people mean in business when they say ' I can't seem to get focused on the key tasks and get the important jobs finished!' Space probe!

As you embark on this massive clear up, a word of warning. When you clear space, the natural tendency will be to refill that space very quickly, almost without noticing that it's happening. Some of this is because although we have created the physical space, our new habits haven't yet developed and so we work in the old regimes and lo and behold we're soon cluttered again! There are two significant steps you must take in order for this whole Order principle to work.

Firstly, the universe doesn't like vacuums. It fills them. So when you clear out, your subconscious also becomes uncluttered. In order to ensure it fills with the right material, you must use the mindchanger techniques described in Principle Five to fill the vacuum.

Secondly, your new regime must include a maintenance programme. Include a 'clear desk' routine at the end of the working day. If you have to do your own filing, have a filing routine. Better to do all the filing once during the week rather than every day! This saves time. So you'll need a 'Filing Tray' close at hand, where everything goes ready for the filing session. Similarly, having a Reading Tray allows you to do all your reading and study at one session during the week rather than trying to study and keep up to date with industry and business issues every day. We'll talk more about this when we cover Organisation. Maintaining a clear, uncluttered work area is a small but significant way of maintaining focus. Make it easy to do, and easy to maintain.

FART on your paperwork

There are only 4 things you can do with paperwork.

File
Act
Refer
Trash

File: for easy retrieval at a later date because the information is valuable. File in terms of 'where will I look for this later when I need it?' rather than 'where can I file this?'

Act: understanding that you won't necessarily act upon it right now, but that you have a system for acting on these things based on your prioritising.

Refer: to someone else to deal with. But again with a system, depending on relative importance, of following up ongoing actions.

Trash: system = the bin.

And you can use the same mnemonic for your email Inbox.

For Inbox control set a target, daily, for the number of unattended messages which are allowed to languish overnight. And weekly go back to zero – use FART. Book a session for dealing with this as part of your weekly organisation session.

Organisation

After ordering the past/present, it's time to organise for the present/future. It might sound obvious, but your organisation needs to reflect where you want to get to and the regimes you want to deploy to get there. Many a time, I have seen people getting organised around things which have little or no bearing on their result areas.

This whole area is about creating 'enabling structures' which keep you operating at your most effective where you need to be. It's about understanding your very own 80/20 rule, and applying it so that you maximise your involvement and effectiveness in those activities within your 20 percent which produce the 80 percent of the results you are looking for. It's about leveraging your time, your focus, your financial resources.

It's also about systemising the 80 percent of your routine activity so you can focus on your true talents and abilities which really make the most difference to a business activity. This approach will produce breakthroughs. For example, instead of spending 80 percent of your time when preparing for a business client meeting doing all those things you routinely do for every meeting of that sort, you focus your time on those things which will really make the meeting a massive success. Working on proposed solutions and preparing great questions to ask, and how you are going to answer their great questions. In order to do this, the routine tasks need to be taken out of your sphere of involvement as much as possible – either by delegating them, or by having a checklist which reduces the amount of your own 'personal hard drive' given over to thinking about them. Checklists can be the most fundamental systems in a business, but so few people really use them.

Okay, so now think of all the routine tasks which are involved in your key areas. If you run a professional service practice (e.g. solicitors, accountants, financial advisers, therapists, consultants, and so on), you will spend lots of time meeting clients, and this will be a key area to perform at your peak. But I see so many professional people poorly prepared, and inevitably rushed with this key activity. So for you, there will be a number of tasks which revolve around this activity which are relatively routine and which do not require your professional brain power. So a series of standardised checklists would help here, allowing you to ensure you gave a high level of service every time.

So, for your business, where could you use checklists?

Let's just consider this in the big picture. Consider a business growth strategy:

The four ways to grow a business

The Guerrilla business person knows this – there are only four ways to grow a business. So, if what you are doing doesn't fit in with these categories, then you should not be doing it.

1. Increase the **number of customers**
2. Increase the **value of each transaction**
3. Increase the **frequency of transactions**
4. Increase the **effectiveness of systems** within the business

If we do only one, two or three of these, the chances are that we will not grow at the speed we want. We need to work on all four simultaneously in order to have a massive impact on the results we are achieving.

So a business with 100 customers, each transacting £1,000 worth of business with us twice per year gives us a turnover as follows:

Number of customers	100
Value of each transaction	1000
Frequency of transactions	2
= Total Turnover	200,000

Now let's increase that by 10 per cent across all three areas.

Number of customers	110
Value of each transaction	1100
Frequency	2.2
= Total Turnover	266,620

This represents an increase of 33 per cent. Now let's increase all three by 25 per cent over the initial figures

Number of customers	125
Value	1250
Frequency	2.5
= Total turnover	390,000

an increase of 95 per cent.

And what of step 4, increasing the effectiveness of the systems in the business? Well, without this element, the growth will not be sustained, the new capacity not delivered and the new levels of attractiveness for our product/service not maintained. Which means our clients won't feel that they are getting service and value (and therefore will not want to pay our prices) and won't keep coming back (frequency).

And so this is where to bring the principle of organisation to bear.

Similarly, this is where to employ the Japanese principle of Kaizen – Continuous Improvement. This is about taking small steps forward in each area and measuring the improvement before then fully implementing the new change. It's about being one percent better in a hundred things and continually developing these systems through ongoing improvement.

The Business Function Circuit

Do you sometimes feel that you are over-organising your business? Are you organising the right things?

Many businesses have organisation and administrative functions which do not actually relate to the key result areas of the business (namely the strategic, marketing, operations and financial functions). Remember this is about functions, not number of people, or even necessarily about departments. Even a one-man business has all these functions.

Does your business have a simple circuit like the following? Or do you have lots of admin activity and organising which does nothing to support the business in terms of what it actually delivers to its customers? This is often the case where businesses have seen lots of change through the years but have lots of tasks which 'we've always done this way'.

For many small businesses and large organisations alike, this can be crippling, amounting to paralysis in some cases.

Here is a circuit to work on.

The Business Function Circuit

System Requirements

How much should be standardised?

Even though I'm a sole trader/small business, organising the right things is crucial to the delivery of outstanding service results. In fact, because I have fewer people working for me, having these systems will ensure more effective performance.

So, which Functions need a system, or can have a system?

Marketing	Operations	Financial
✓ ✓ ✓ ✓ ✓ ✓ ✓ ✓ ✓ ✓ ✓ ✓		

Therefore, I need to have the following checklists/systems:

System/checklist	To be in place by
1	
2	
3	
4	
5	
6	
7	
8	
9	
10	
11	
12	

Personal organisation

There are some areas of personal organisation which will have an enormous bearing on your success. But again, rather like the Mars Space Probe, it's the seemingly simple things which are often overlooked. For example, do you have all the things you need to have readily accessible in your office? Does your work area help or hinder you? Do the trays you have reflect the work you do?

Trays

For so long, the traditional approach has an IN tray, a PENDING tray, and an OUT tray. Is this the best format for you? Does it really reflect the segments of work that make up your Key Result Areas? Why not have a set of trays which reflect the regime you are building – a daily diet representing all aspects of your work. For example:

- **ON tray** (for planning work, literally working ON your business)
- **Meeting preps tray** (if your business revolves around meetings)
- **Meetings ready tray**
- **Post-meeting tray** (once you return from a meeting the file goes here with a list of after-actions noted on the front)
- **Reading/Study tray**
- **Phone calls to make tray**
- **Calling me back tray** (for those people who you have called, but who are going to call you back, either because they weren't available, or because the ball has been left in their court over some issue or other). Paperclip the outline of what you were calling about to the outside of the file, and that way you will easily remember ALL of the items for discussion immediately they call back)
- **Delegation trays** – to put things for others to deal with
- **Filing Tray**
- **And a TODAY tray** – This is where you put all those items which are both Urgent and Important. This is your Quadrant 1 tray.

The TODAY tray is the only tray which should be on your desk (preferably it should be off the desk but closest to hand).

It is fed by the other trays daily according to the balance regime you have in place. So if you need to conduct on average three meetings per day, then you also need to prepare three meetings per day (some may only need minor preparation, of course, whilst some will require full proposals and reports), and you will need to do all the follow-up actions/post-meeting work on three meetings per day. That way you never face an insurmountable back-log. Some people have a regime which allows them to prepare for all their week's meetings in one go, and also do all the after-meeting work for the week in one go.

The message is, have a routine and a regular regime.

The Magic Timetable

This is a weekly regime, with all the time slots allocated for a successful and very effective week. It represents the ultimate regime, the 'ideal'. OK, so you aren't going to be perfect – and let's face it that's not what we are aiming for. The timetable simply creates awareness of what you are doing versus what you could be doing, and will eradicate any bad habits and wasted time. It will confront you with decisions over the use of your time rather than have you simply slip through the day only to find yourself at 6pm saying 'I don't know where the day went!'

The timetable template might look like this. Then simply allocate your activities for the entire week. Imagine what a school pupil would do without his or her timetable. So why shouldn't the professional business person have something similar. And why not extend the idea to all areas of your life. Now, before you think it's inflexible, let me reiterate – the purpose of this is to create time awareness, and to show you that in fact you do have time in the week to do all the things you would like, as long as you get organised. It may also highlight to you if you are trying to put too much into the week, beyond the realms of physical possibility. This way, you choose what to leave out, based on your priorities, and not simply left to chance.

The Magic Timetable

	Monday	Tuesday	Wednesday	Thursday	Friday	Saturday	Sunday
7.15am							
7.45am							
8.30am							
9.00am							
12.30pm							
1.30pm							
4.30pm							
5.00pm							
7.00pm							
9.00pm							
10.30pm							

Action Lists

Or 'To finish' lists. Not 'To do' lists. The 'To do' list represents the language of victim – having things you *must* do. The alternative 'Action List' conjures up a different image entirely.

Most people agree that having an action list, in some form, improves their productivity on any day. Most people have been on a course where they have learned how to make up an action list. They understand prioritisation. They understand the importance, psychologically, of ticking things off the list as the day progresses. They have even felt the satisfaction, at the end of the working day, of knowing that all the most crucial tasks received their full attention and were completed. But:

- 87 percent of executives only very rarely use an action list
- 10 percent will occasionally use an action list
- and 3 percent use an action list on most days (i.e. more than 3 times a week).

Do those numbers ring any bells? 87, 10, 3.

Haven't we seen them somewhere before?

The Daily Stratagram

This Stratagram allows us to make our 'Action List' a more compelling mechanism. With practice, it will help you move with ease through the productive activities of the day. There is no doubt that it owes a lot to the work of Stephen Covey who developed a concept of awareness with his Time Quadrants, and to other time effectiveness techniques which I have amalgamated onto one easy-to-use tool which will enhance your focus in performing daily tasks which are consistent with your goals and objectives.

Covey's Time Quadrants provide us with a Time Awareness concept recognising that Time Management is a myth. You can't manage time, you can only manage what you do in the time available

– it's about scheduling and priority awareness rather than simply cramming lots of small tasks into the day.

Imagine four quadrants as follows:

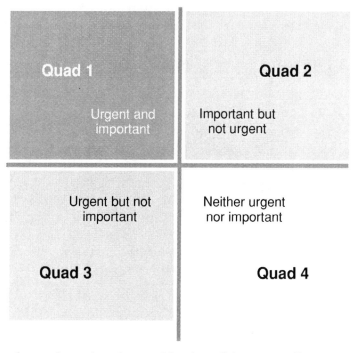

All tasks can be assigned a combination of the two attributes:

Urgent: those things which are pressing upon us
Important: those things which attach to our goals and objectives.

So, we can have tasks which are both pressing upon us, and also relate to our objectives (quadrant 1). And so on. If you imagine quadrant one tasks are firefighting tasks, whilst quadrant two tasks are fire prevention, you have the idea.

The secret is to move the focus to spending more time in Quadrant 2.

On its own, this is a fantastic way to become aware of the need to spend more time on the most important issues. Indeed I recommend you have this put on a card with the question 'which quadrant are you currently working in?' underneath it, and display this somewhere prominently in your office.

The Daily Stratagram uses this concept to help create a Daily Action plan which also pays attention to prioritising what is on your 'to do' list. Depending on your working style, the stratagram could be used weekly, rather than daily, to enable you to see on one page how to allocate your focus for the week ahead.

Use it to write the various tasks on your list into the appropriate quadrants. Once you have done this, you simply feed the central section (the morning question and key result areas) to produce a very focused list of priorities for the day. These take priority over all else. I have found that for Quadrant 2 a 'Mindmap' is the most appropriate way of developing the task list, as many of the items here will fall into the realms of larger more strategic projects where a number of different smaller actions will go to make up one area of activity. The quadrants are different sizes in order to reflect the amount of time which should be spent in them. But don't forget, this is simply a tool and you should feel free to adapt it in whatever way you like.

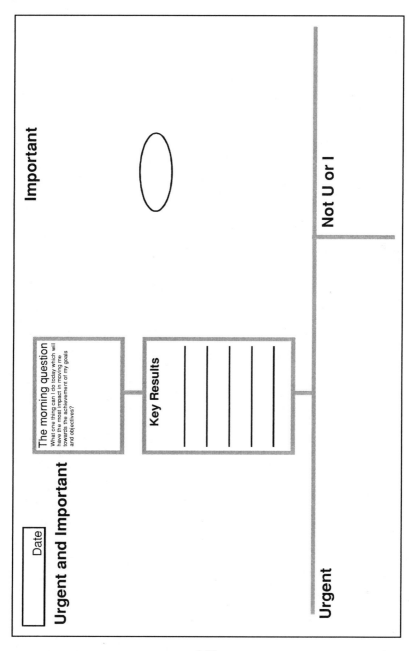

Don't be put off by the apparent complexity of the daily Stratagram. It is far easier to operate than it may first appear. And it is very worth pursuing and practising with. However, because the finished Daily Stratagram looks complicated, you may prefer a simpler method.

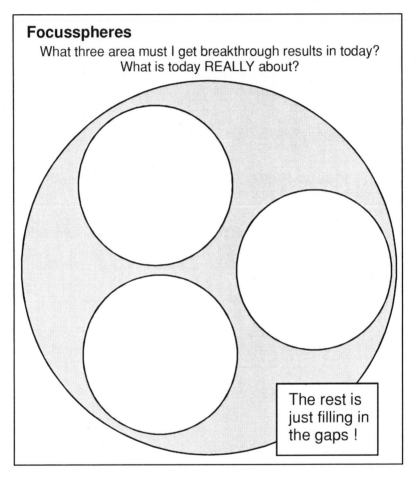

Focusspheres

What three area must I get breakthrough results in today?
What is today REALLY about?

The rest is just filling in the gaps !

Put the areas of focus in the internal circles, and everything else outside these three circles, but inside the large oval shape. This indicates where your three key result tasks are for the day, and is a graphic reminder that all other items are at the edges.

Setting up the day

Let's just run through the setting up the day scenario just to show you how all this works.

The day starts the night before. A ten minute session, finishing up today, clearing the desk, and preparing a list of all the things to be done tomorrow – but not yet putting priorities on them.

Next morning

- Around the trays, create the **today tray**
- **Mindchangers**
- **Daily stratagram** – this is where you prioritise (and very important therefore that it comes just after mindchangers).
- **Prime Time** – includes your **Golden Hour** when at your most effective and doing those things which are most important.

And so on through your day, using the daily stratagram to focus attention where it counts.

During the day, you'll encounter interruptions and also additional work or tasks which you hadn't anticipated. So all you need to do is ask 'Is this more important than what I'm currently doing?' If not, then continue with the current task until complete and then assess where the new task should fit in the order of the day (or if it can simply be put aside for tomorrow or sometime in the future).

Many people might look at this approach and feel it is a long-winded way of getting organised for the day. But let's look at the alternative; and I suspect this version may ring some bells with you.

Arrive at work. Coffee. Check emails and phone messages. Work through them. First meeting of the day. After meeting, check phone messages (and emails). Work through them. And so on.

The difference? Control.

A different approach would be used for your planning days.

Hotel Days – Monthly Planning Days – Weekly Organisation

171

Days/ Self-Organisation Sessions. They will all have their own regular agendas – but again the weekly organisation day/self-organisation session is based around the Tray system. For example:

Weekly Organisation Day Agenda

Finishing current week:
> Any follow-ups to meetings
> Any follow-ups to phone calls
> Clear IN tray (FART)
> Clear reading / study tray
> Clear Filing Tray
> Clear/check delegation tray
> FART on Inbox
> Strategic phone calls to allies – update

Setting up Next week:
> Preps for meetings
> Key tasks for the coming week
> > -Opportunities
> > -Marketing
> > -Current projects

Self coaching session – personal performance debrief, success log (see Principle 8 R&R)

Team Briefing

Time to get Organised

> *'If I had eight hours to cut down a tree,*
> *I would spend six of them sharpening the saw.'*
> > Abraham Lincoln

It's an old chestnut that people don't have time to get organised. But of course they do.

We all do. You do.

It's not so much lack of time in getting organised, but lack of understanding as to the importance of being organised.

And this is born out of the fact that when most people devote time to getting organised, they tend to organise the wrong things. This leads to a feeling that the whole task was simply 'nice to do' or the icing on the cake, rather than being of any actual value in developing the business. And we subconsciously tell ourselves that it's a task which we should really only be doing when there's nothing else to deal with. And of course, in the modern business world such a window of opportunity never arrives.

Many years ago, starting out in business, I was fortunate to be introduced to a wonderful book by Frank Bettger, *'How I raised myself from failure to success in selling'*. In it, he reproduces a poem by Douglas Malloch which encapsulates the conundrum perfectly.

There may be little wrong with you,
The way you live, the work you do,
But I can very plainly see
Exactly what is wrong with me.
It isn't that I'm indolent
Or dodging duty by intent;
I work as hard as anyone,
And yet I get so little done.

The morning goes, the noon is here,
Before I know, the night is near,
And all around me, I regret,
Are things I haven't finished yet.
If I could just get organised!
I oftentimes have realised
Not all that matters is the man;
The man must also have a plan.

With you, there may be nothing wrong,
But here's my trouble right along;
I do the things that don't amount
To very much, of no account,
That really seem important though
And let a lot of matters go.
I nibble this, I nibble that,
But never finish what I'm at.
I work as hard as anyone,
And yet, I get so little done,
I'd do so much you'd be surprised,
If I could just get organised.

Time to Download:

Remember – this is not a chance just to write down things that have been confirmed, but more importantly new things that have been learned.

If you have been reminded of something that you knew but had never done anything about, it can be classed as newly learned. 'To know and not to do, is not to know.'

Action Zone

What I have learned so far ...

What I am going to do about it/use from now on ...

11

The Seventh Principle –
Shop Window

The next planet: URANUS

In Holst's famous Planet Suite, Uranus is described as The Magician

There appears to be a 'magic' X Factor common to successful people – something akin to Charisma and Luck. We often hear the term 'they always come up smelling of roses!'

And it's a trait developed at an unconscious level as well. On the face of it, it's an indescribable, intangible quality which cannot be copied.

Is it that being cheery, positive, charismatic (whatever that is?) or attractive leads to success? Or is it that success creates these attributes? 'Of course they're happy – I would be happy, positive and enthusiastic if I had their luck and money!' A bit of a 'Chicken and egg'.

Napoleon famously asked of senior staff officers before he appointed them into positions such as Corps Commander, Divisional Commander or Brigade Commander 'Est il heureux?' which means 'Is he lucky?' but literally translates as 'Is he happy?' Perhaps that's where the phrase 'Happy-go-lucky' comes from! Certainly he recognised the link between success and having a knack of creating luck.

Whatever the link, once all the previous principles have been adopted and are being utilised, to a great extent this principle follows naturally. You will have an attractive 'Shop Window' if you have high self esteem (Inner Vision), are oriented on a journey you want to take in life and are living a design (Future Now and Master Plan), and so on.

But as well as the unconscious signals being reflected in your shop window, there are some significant conscious steps you can take, and techniques you can employ, to maximise the shop window effect. You can essentially make yourself more attractive, and therefore attract more of what you want. Largely this whole principle is about communication (both verbal and non-verbal), direct and indirect, and which is the outward sign of what you stand for – a personal brand.

It's also about marketing – personal marketing. But don't make the mistake of applying this principle to a business and thinking that the principle is JUST about marketing, or that marketing is JUST about this principle. A complete marketing plan and a robust marketing engine is about employing ALL of the principles – Future Now, Planning, Persistent Progression, Mindset, Order & Organisation (marketing systems), Rehearsal & Renewal (principle 8, and especially Kaizen, which we'll come to shortly), and yes, Shop Window. So marketing is a function, just as any other function, where the application of all the principles will create success.

So, how can we develop this attractiveness? Well, there are a number of key tools to consciously apply which make your 'Shop Window' stand out from the rest of the 'shops on the High street of life'.

The first is Enthusiasm. Being passionate and deeply involved and interested in life. If you can't get excited about you, how can you expect anyone else to? Ralph Waldo Emerson said: 'Nothing great was ever achieved in life without enthusiasm'. The Big E. But most people are at best disinterested in their own lives and their own work to the extent that they seek refuge in the world of soap opera TV to create interest! Now, I'm not having a go at soap operas here. But I am amazed at how so many people spend more time being interested in the lives of the characters on TV than in the lives of real people around them – let alone in their own lives! Most people at work appear only 5 percent present. They are not concentrating or really 'Being There' for their clients, their colleagues, their bosses, or their subordinates. They have lost the will to excel. As Michael Gerber says, their businesses have become 'killing fields of the spirit'!

'Life is too short for non-Wow projects!' as Tom Peters says.

If you aren't making your life a project which is full of 'Wow', full of power and enjoyment, then how can you expect others to be attracted to you? You can't. And the outward expression of your joy, delight, excitement, passion for your life is your 'Shop Window'.

Are you standing out as 'Extra-ordinary'? Is it a life-impacting experience to meet you? Or at the very least a high-point in the day?

This whole principle is about reflecting something more then 'Average'. It's about living a **better-than-satisfactory** life, a better than 'Satisfactory' business, better than 'Satisfactory' relationships, better than 'Satisfied' clients and customers. It's about creating a 'Great' life.

Has anyone ever heard of 'Alexander the Average'?

Act enthusiastic to be enthusiastic

In order to be enthusiastic, you must first *act* enthusiastic. You must consciously act with the posture, look, smile of an enthusiast.

In so doing, you transmit a signal to yourself that you are enthusiastic – even if at first you are only 'acting' it. Our body posture and physiology reflects our state of mind. And so in order to create a new state of mind, we can use our physiology. Each grade on our own enthusiasm scale has a matching posture. These are inescapably linked. Most people, without realising it, allow their state of mind to dictate their posture. But if we consciously want to upgrade our state of mind, we can do so by upgrading our posture, physiology, even dress and appearance. The fact that we are 'ACTING' enthusiastic sends a signal to our mind to be enthusiastic. And it's the same with the words we use.

> '*A man without a smiling face must not open a shop.*'
> Chinese proverb

So choose your attitude. Attitude is purely a function of perspective. People's attitude can be altered depending on the perspective. And, we tend to develop a negative attitude when we lose our perspective. Now, I'm not talking about the sort of Blind Optimism which is often mistakenly associated with the Americanised (sorry, guys – but you know what I mean), almost evangelical Positive Mental Attitude brigade.

Initially, choosing your attitude is a conscious discipline. But after a while, it becomes a habit, and therefore part of the Mindset which we talked about in Principle Five. A mindset which will support us and allow us to see opportunities where others see only obstacles.

Choosing your attitude

At the Start of each day, just as you choose the clothes you will wear, Choose your attitude. Make a *conscious* decision – and match this by deliberately 'acting' the part of that enthusiastic person.

Match your physiology!

179

A bullet-proof 'Shop Window'

In developing a 'Shop Window' that clearly displays your values and what you stand for, you will want to make it 'Bullet-proof'.

In other words, you will need to 'walk the talk' and clearly demonstrate what you are about. I'm not talking about being perfect here. I'm talking about being congruent, meaningful and consistent with your values.

This comes through your shop window communication to produce a genuine reflection. Many people create a façade that allows them to manipulate and influence in the worst forms. Many people use communication tools in a manipulative way (thinking they are developing a shop window) to gain short term results, which is why this principle (just as all the other principles) must not stand alone. In the same way that any tool can be used to manipulate for good or ill, the Shop Window can be a genuine attractiveness born out of a willingness to achieve a win:win result for all parties to a business relationship; or it can be a weapon to manipulate. The difference is in the motive. And by now you will realise that with all the other principles in attendance, the motive will have undergone considerable checks and balances along the way.

Similarly, being 'attractive' is also NOT about being a 'nice guy' who is easy to do business with – something which can be equally damaging and lead to a lose:win. If either you or they feel manipulated, it won't work.

The shop window is about projecting a decisiveness and certainty which is attractive to those who can create a Win:Win, and is unattractive to anyone else.

Many companies set out Visions and Values statements, but forget to develop all their behaviours as consistent with this. This can be at the very top of any organisation right through to the foot of the company. It is about displaying integrity through action – and it's sometimes the little actions which if not congruent with the stated values and visions will shatter the Shop Window, both internally with the rest of the team, and externally with clients and customers. We hear about salespeople who profess a high degree of professionalism and service but who wear shoddy, unpolished shoes and 'Mickey Mouse' watches, and use chewed up biros, and wear 'Tasmanian Devil' ties. I'm sure you get the drift. Something just doesn't sit right and the customer does not necessarily feel confident in what they are being told. The customer may not be aware consciously of this feeling, but they will have a sense that something doesn't add up.

Black and White Thinking

The whole concept is about standing for something or falling for everything, and letting everyone you meet know as much as possible about what you do stand for by the nature of your Shop Window.

Black and White thinking is the ability to remove the clutter from your communication in order that the prospective buyer of your product (you) can see clearly what he or she is looking at. So help them to make the decision by being decisive yourself.

The ability to project this certainty and commitment comes from our Vision and our values. The shop window is in fact a window onto these values and this certainty of direction and vision. It shows that you are courageous, committed, decisive. The shop window creates a transparent attractiveness. There is no need to pull the wool, or flatter to deceive. There are too many 'Gonna Doers' out there. Don't be a 'Gonna' otherwise you'll be a Gone-r (as in dead) – particularly in the fast-moving world of modern business.

So send out messages about your Black & White thinking through the Shop Window.

As an example, one of my favourite observations concerns the use of the word 'Try'. By saying 'I'll try to do xyz' we give ourselves a get-out for what we believe will happen, i.e. that we will fail to actually do it.

Imagine you have just asked someone if they are doing to make it to a party on Friday evening. Their answer, 'I'll try and be there.' You know, and they know, that the likelihood of them actually turning up is slim.

Similarly, when we say, 'at the moment, the firm is trying to push ahead with xyz', we are courting failure to actually do it. And we are believing we won't actually achieve the desired result, but we've been brought up to the paradigm 'no one can blame you if you've tried your best'. True. So we are saying we are not to blame for the upcoming failure.

'Try' removal always improves the power of the message.

Fine Fines

And then there is, of course, the word 'fine', as in 'How are you?' 'Fine!'

Oh dear. Is that all you can muster? But it's a habitual reaction.

The same goes for 'alright' or 'not bad', the latter being particularly destructive.

And the reason the latter is particularly destructive is that the mind cannot discern negatives and so it just thinks of 'bad'. For example, if I say to you, 'whatever you do, don't think of a cool ice cream', what's the first thing that pops into your mind's eye. Yes. Bold as anything, a cool ice cream. But I said don't think of one! It's the same with 'not bad'. To be able to conceive ,not bad,, the mind first has to think of 'bad'.

In fact, I have observed that 87 percent of people who receive a greeting respond with 'Fine', 'Not Bad', or 'Alright.'

Ten percent will immediately launch into a diatribe as to why it's a bad day to be on the planet. They will recount all their ills, or those of others around them, or the weather, government, boss, clients and so on. It's awful. How does that sound as a 'Shop Window' ?

It's those people who say something different here who immediately build stronger relationships through having an attractive shop window.

Imagine if you replied 'Great!' instead. See what happens. It firstly shows you care enough about their question to give a proper answer, and not just the ordinary response. And so, what happens when you reciprocate the question 'And how are you?' Well you are telling them that you really do care about the answer and aren't just opening the conversation in the normal, average, boring way.

It is a fact that people prefer to associate with successful people. So transmitting success in our initial engagement, our opening gambit, is crucial – and it's a habit which can be developed just like any other habit.

So create a 'Fine Fine' for yourself (fining yourself for saying 'Fine') which works on the same lines as a swear box and will soon have you replacing these words with better alternatives.

Communication

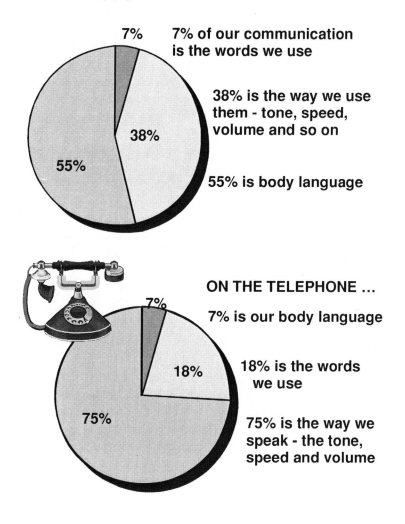

7%

7% of our communication is the words we use

38% is the way we use them - tone, speed, volume and so on

38%

55%

55% is body language

ON THE TELEPHONE ...

7% is our body language

18% is the words we use

18%

75%

75% is the way we speak - the tone, speed and volume

Your Shop Window communication is at both the verbal and non-verbal level. It also includes written and telephone communication, as these two areas are often your first point of contact with prospective customers of your 'product'.

In many cases, businesses and the people on the front-line of these businesses are unaware of how poor a shop window they are portraying. 'It is all transaction and no interaction' as my friend Barry Hilton would say.

Those companies who thrive manage to make the whole process of doing business with them an enjoyable experience – starting with an attractive shop window. And similarly those people who thrive do so by making their lives attractive to others, and attractive to themselves. Too many people trail about looking as if they are really not enjoying their time here one bit!

The Telephone Shop Window

It always amazes me how many people stutter and splutter when confronted by an answer-phone or voice-mail system. And yet, so many of these prevail in business today (and in all our lives). So it should come as no surprise when you come across one. So be ready to leave your message. And if it's an area you find difficult, then having a pre-prepared message which you are well practised with is the answer. And make it powerful. Don't forget, the person you are leaving the message for will be faced with lots of calls to return, so yours needs to stand out.

Similarly, when devising your own answer-phone or voice-mail message, make it powerful and remember it's your shop window. Include a promise to return their call within a certain timescale (and make sure you do return the call), and include a tag-line if you run a business – 'Thank you for calling xyz limited, home of the abc product.' Always let your shop window work for you.

Dynamic Voice Message

**There will be five messages on their voice-
mail. So, what will make mine stand out as the
one they feel they want to return first?**

- **Stand Up – straight**
- **Picture them hearing your voice**
- **Smile**

Hello _____ (their name)

This is _____

Message (short and to the point) _____

_____

My number is _____

That's _____ (repeat number)

Thank you, _____ (their name)

The Cocktail Party Gambit

The world of business is full of networking opportunities, and most
people in business use this as a key element in their marketing engine.
But many fail to make full use of the networking situations they put
themselves in.

Getting it right when you are networking is all about the way you
use your shop window. And it's the initial attractiveness of your shop
window which will engage or not.

'What do you do?'

Your opening gambit must be attractive, using powerful words. It must be enthusiastic. It must be meaningful to them. 'What do you do?' can become a way of exploring 'what can you do for me?' if you answer with a powerful opening gambit. Remember, that so many people go to network solely thinking 'what can I get from this?' Of course there are those who attend lunches and breakfasts with the mindset of 'what can I give?', but they are truly few and far between. So if many of the people you encounter are essentially in 'me mode', you must engage them in those terms. Not what you do, but what you can do for them. What is it that they want to buy? What appeals to them and their key need/want.

And as we all know I am sure, listening to the other party is critical. Don't spend the whole session talking about you. Successful people are great listeners. Ask people about their business. And don't fall into the trap of talking about the past. A very powerful opening gambit might be, 'Tell me about your Business Foreground.' In other words, get interested in what is occupying their attention right now, and where their immediate challenges lie, and what they are currently excited about. That will be the key to how you might be able to immediately help them – either yourself directly, or by introducing them to someone else who may just have the secret to unlock their current problems.

When asked, 'what do you do?' have your cocktail party gambit so well rehearsed that it trips off the tongue in a powerful and engaging way. Practice it, polish it, and you will never stumble at the critical moment. Your shop window will attract.

Cocktail party gambit

Describe in 17 words what you do, in terms of direct end benefit which your customers receive.

Learn this, and learn it well.

And also have a range of around three great questions which you can ask in a fresh and compelling way to find out about others.

This will allow you to concentrate on their answers, and really listen, rather than constantly thinking, 'what am I going to say next?' which is what so many people are doing when networking.

Time to Download:

Remember – this is not a chance just to write down things that have been confirmed, but more importantly new things that have been learned.

If you have been reminded of something that you knew but had never done anything about, it can be classed as newly learned. 'To know and not to do, is not to know.'

Action Zone

What I have learned so far ...

What I am going to do about it/use from now on ...

12

The Eighth Principle – R&R: Rehearsal and Renewal

> **Our next planet: NEPTUNE**
>
> Like the waters of the seas and oceans, the business world and the lives we lead are forever changing, constantly moving, and we must always be updating. Which is why we must continually revisit our principles and our success habits - to refresh and renew, and rehearse constant improvement.

The best antidote to the FTI syndrome (Failure To Implement) is to stay FIT (Fully In Tune – i.e. with no 'Interference').

Staying fit is all about constant rehearsal and renewal. This whole principle is about the pursuit of excellence as a journey, not perfection as a destination.

Successful people always seek personal and professional improvement. This is a constant and ongoing process. The renewal of the goals and vision every day (e.g. through use of the Mindsetting techniques) and the regular development and practising and training as we work on our performance.

Of all the forms of rehearsal which will have the most impact, rehearsing the outcome to a given situation in your mind as a 'fait accompli' is the most powerful. Creating a belief in our ability to perform by tricking our subconscious into believing it has already happened is a tool used by many top professional sports people before a match. But the rehearsal doesn't stop there. The continuous development of professional skills is critical in the 'knowledge economy'. However, it's often the so called soft skills which are most neglected. Why? Because they are actually the hard skills to develop because their performance rests on habits, and normally improvement involves first of all removing old habits. Which is why, although they spend millions on upgrading IT hardware and software packages, most companies have huge viruses and are running on old outmoded software in the biggest computers in the business – the computers between the ears of themselves and their workers.

The whole of military life revolves around constant rehearsal of a situation which we should hope will never arrive. All of the training, procedures, drills and discipline is designed to create a machine which will excel when put to the ultimate test. These elements nurture the military team mindset. Everything is about being geared up and ready to go for that ultimate test of capability. But it can only be done through training, drills, drills, drills and more drills.

In the same way, in business, we need to be continually rehearsing our performance, perfecting our skills. And often it's about repetition of the basics, rather than constantly looking for the new-fangled shortcut route.

'To know and not to do, is not to know.'

Absolutely true. Often in business we know the things we should be doing to succeed, but we don't do them. This is as bad as not knowing them in the first place. For example, the struggling Sales Executive who is simply not putting in the productive activity required. Not making the calls. Yes, he or she knows that making the calls is the route to success. But in not making the calls he is nullifying that knowledge. In fact, it's worse than that, because there is a link between the calls and success. The converse is a subliminal link between not making calls and Failure! i.e. knowing and not doing doesn't create a neutral result. The outcome is decidedly detrimental. When we don't do what we know we should be doing, as well as we should be doing it, we tell ourselves that we cannot succeed. The call-reluctant sales person becomes guilty and deflects any other routes to success. The spiral is endless.

So we need to have around us constant reminders which allow us to renew our commitment and vision and capabilities, and to rehearse our professional skills.

What form should these reminders take?

Well, we've already seen the power of mindsetting-style techniques such as the Star.

But you can also create reminders which appeal specifically to your own sensory preference. If you happen to be very visual, then visual props are the answer. Pictures representing the success principles, along with visual reminders, quotes and so on may be most useful. If you are kinaesthetic, the Elastic Banned idea below will help.

Elastic banned

This is a means of banishing any negative thoughts or removing any old habits which need to be replaced with new ways of thinking or acting. It's a way of banning certain thoughts or actions.

Simply put an elastic band around your wrist. Whenever you accidentally revert to the old habit or way of thinking, simply give the elastic band a flick – strong enough to act as a reminder. Don't feel as if you have to inflict huge pain for this to work. The association is enough, and after a very short time you become aware of the bad habit. You can then make a conscious decision to replace it each time, until it becomes a new good habit.

Kaizen

The Japanese art of 'Continuous Improvement' is about being one percent better in a hundred things rather than one hundred percent better in one thing.

It's about gradually making improvements in lots of areas in order to create a larger overall improvement. And the principle of R&R applies here, whether it's a business improvement plan, or a personal improvement plan. Kaizen has certainly most often been associated with business development. It is about taking one area for improvement, creating a new way of acting (a new system, for example), measuring the performance of the new way against the results you were getting under the old system. If the new way is better, it's about implementing this as the revised way of performing. Then back to innovating on this revised method to again find an even better way. And so on.

Personal/Professional development using Kaizen

Yes, of course this can be applied to individual improvement. But business owners and large organisations – BEWARE.

When you encourage your best executives to improve themselves, you must be prepared for the outcome, and you must build 'Maximum Headroom' into the organisation. Too often I have seen middle/senior executives develop themselves professionally, only to become frustrated at the lack of vision, change and development at the top of the company. The result? Of course, they become embittered and worse, they leave. So your best people who you have invested most time, energy and money in training and developing move to pastures new. The solution – always stretch the top tier as well.

So, R&R is about constant reminders of your Values, Vision, Goals, and the tools and techniques for effectiveness to make sure that you keep developing in the direction you want to go.

Many people find that they operate best when they are in some way recording their activity through a journal diary, or in some other way. I have certainly produced my own weekly self coaching reminder sheet which allows me to record the big wins each week whilst at the same time keeping some key tools at the front of my mind, and ensuring I am employing the principles – especially where I have set a particular Persistent Progression in process, or where I am operating a 28 day Grid. Each week, having a self-coaching half hour to round off the week, say on a Friday afternoon, provides a structure to your R&R. So use the self-coaching session sheet to be as objective as possible about this, otherwise you will tend to allow your judgement of your own performance to be too harsh and self-critical or too soft and not stretching enough.

The Self Coaching Session Sheet

Date

Best thing this week

Checklist

❑ Goals revisited

Highlights and Business 'Victories'

❑ Mindsetter
   techniques used
    Star
✓
    Lift
✓
    Cards
✓
    Train
✓
    Time travel talk
✓

❑ Daily stratagram
✓

❑ Key Results Areas

❑ Health fitness

Personal Action Plan Progress (eg. Ref
  energy
Tactical Targets, ASMs, KSAS,etc)

❑

❑

❑

❑

New Issues and Lessons

❑

For the Coming Week:

Improvement commitments

Focus

194

It can be no coincidence that so many successful people keep a journal-style diary. They record events of significance, feelings, improvements and successes along the way, creating a story unfolding – the story of their life.

But, writing a daily journal may appear a chore if you have never done it before. Again, it's about habit. But if you don't intend to form this habit, maybe an alternative will create the same result. I know of at least one person who records on audio tape a one-minute summary at the end of each day. Or you could do a video diary. Make it easy to do. But certainly have some form of record to provide a sense of your journey of significance rather than the whole of life and business being a blur with no apparent purpose. The journal will also improve your powers of observation of all the little things which happen to you and which you make happen which provide life with its rich pattern.

Also, keeping a log of improvements in key result areas professionally is critical to ongoing improvement. For example, if one of your key performance areas is having meetings with prospective clients, have a debrief sheet which will help you note down what went well and what needs improvement or reminding.

This is not about being 'perfect', as that will drive you to distraction and into areas which do not matter. Remember the Pareto principle (80/20) and your Key Result Areas. Remember also the KSAS Stratagram (Knowledge, Skills, Activities, Systems) and focus on making ongoing improvements in relation to these things only. Do not be side-tracked into becoming '100 percent efficient' in areas which ultimately have little or no bearing on the direction you are heading, the goals you have, or the results which are critical to your success. Know when to aim for being the best through ongoing improvement as opposed to being efficient for efficiency's sake.

For example, in the area of ongoing knowledge enhancement, see the Tree of Knowledge opposite.

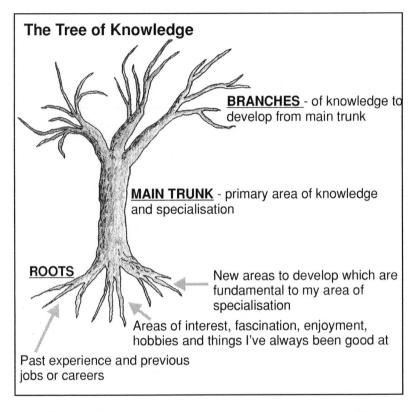

The Tree of Knowledge

BRANCHES - of knowledge to develop from main trunk

MAIN TRUNK - primary area of knowledge and specialisation

ROOTS

New areas to develop which are fundamental to my area of specialisation

Areas of interest, fascination, enjoyment, hobbies and things I've always been good at

Past experience and previous jobs or careers

Each 'Trunk' of knowledge needs to have roots which are sufficiently deep and which allow the knowledge to grow stronger and form branches over time which are off-shoots from the main branch. Don't fall into the trap of planting a 'forest of foundation-less trunks of knowledge'. So choose your fields of expertise (you probably already have the roots based on past areas of experience, areas of fascination and interest, hobbies, previous jobs, and so on). Develop the trunk, and then grow branches from this healthy and deep-rooted tree.

Many people fail to become knowledgeable enough in the areas which matter most, and instead have too broad a range of knowledge, but not deep enough in any one of the most important areas which will improve their effectiveness. The information age means that knowledge is easily and readily available to all. But converting this knowledge into 'know how' which is valuable and helps you achieve what you need to achieve is a very different matter.

Success Logs

Here's a very simple idea that can change the focus of any individual, team, or business. It is also a very practical tool that you can use to help with your R&R.

Most people find it easy to describe all the things which happen which are problems, challenges or areas of weakness which need to be improved. Indeed, most businesses operate suggestion boxes and complaints procedures.

But how many have a Success Log?

We should all celebrate our successes and gain strength from them. But if they aren't being recorded, we too easily forget them. The Success Log should be completed each week, with a simple note describing the nature of the success.

Each person in a team can be encouraged to have at least one item to contribute in this way at the weekly team meeting. What a great way to ensure that in subsequent weeks people are looking for their successes.

Equally, the current week's successes could be recorded as they happen, say on a whiteboard or on colourful cards displayed around the office. The nature of the success doesn't matter. It could be simply learning a new application on a key piece of software for the secretarial team, or for the sales director it could be clinching a new piece of business.

Having used this on many occasions, I can vouch that it works. It certainly has in my coaching practice.

Self-upgrading using the Conscious Triangle

Under The Fifth Principle, we looked at how the subconscious controls and determines most of our performance and behaviour.

But in the conscious arena, we can also make some deliberate upgrades in our habits of performance. And to do this we need to examine three areas. We need to ask 'How can I change the way I perform by enhancing the way I do x, or say y, or think z?' This is a great way of performing a Future Now exercise on our personal performance (à la Principle 2) in order to make a fast and powerful breakthrough in a specific area. An added bonus is that our improvements in this conscious arena help to trigger our subconscious in further developing the powerful mindset we covered in Principle Five.

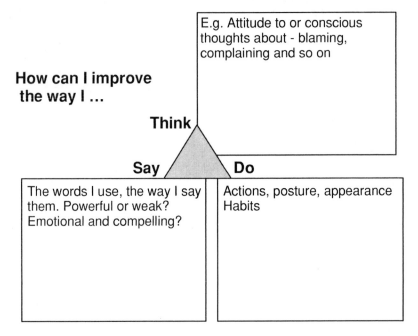

How can I improve the way I ...

Think

E.g. Attitude to or conscious thoughts about - blaming, complaining and so on

Say

The words I use, the way I say them. Powerful or weak? Emotional and compelling?

Do

Actions, posture, appearance Habits

Vital Signs

We must be constantly aware of our own levels of focus, performance and energy. The R& R principle helps us identify early when we have started to hit 'off peak' times. We need to know this before it has detrimental impact, so early warning means you can take early action to make repairs.

I call this **Vital Signs**. Just as a medical professional will see signs of life, and the absence of these signs is a clue to a death, so too we must be able to see our Vital Signs.

For one person who I coach, his fitness regime is a Vital Sign. When he is doing his regime, he knows he is performing well in other areas – business and so on. He also knows that when his fitness regime starts to slacken, it is indicating a slackening of his performance in other areas. It is a symptom of something wider and deeper. So when he notices he is not keeping up his fitness regime, he knows it is time to go into repair mode.

Going into repair mode will mean different things to different people but it is important to take some significant and deliberate action which sends the signal to you that you are carrying out a repair procedure.

For example, going into Vital Sign Repair mode may mean taking a long walk, taking half a day out from business, or rewriting the Mindsetting Cards by upgrading them. Or revisiting your Lifeplan. Or it might be all of these. Decide on your Vital Signs Strategy and be prepared to use it when necessary.

The vital signs

HEAD: 'I can't think straight' or 'I can't think what to do about the next step with ...'
EYES: 'I can't see the way ahead' or 'I can't focus.'
HEART: 'I am not enjoying what I am doing' or 'I am not enthusiastic.'
LUNGS: 'I haven't got the energy to so much as lift a pen.'
ORGANS: 'I don't seem able to get results. I am faced with lots of activity but no productivity.'

First Aid Measures

Head	Clear it. Go for a walk. Revamp your mindset. Mindsetting techniques
Eyes	Refocus on what's important, revisit your goals and reset them. Write your journal or give yourself a 'Pep talk' in writing.
Heart	Do something you like doing. Spend time just for you on a hobby, or watch a favourite film or listen to a favourite piece of music – without guilt – just for you! Buy something just for you. Reward yourself for something you HAVE achieved.
Lungs	Energy. Do something you can accomplish easily. Sometimes having a big clear out can help.
Organs	Action. Some sort of fitness, even just a short walk

OTHT

Part of the R&R Principle is having a process for regularly revisiting our goals, our Prime Vision and our Strategic Objective.

Reading our Mindsetting cards every day is a form of Renewal, as are the other Mindsetting techniques

But it is important to note that as we expand the Mindset Dome, we are in effect moving towards the psychological horizon. So we need to keep opening up beyond it, thereby continually moving the horizon of belief and expectation.

OTHT means **Over The Horizon Targeting**. It is a military term used when a target is in range of a ship's weapons but out of sight, or beyond detection of her radar or other means of detection. The answer is for the warship to send up her helicopter to use its radar to pinpoint the target 'over the horizon'. It feeds information back to the warship which can now target the enemy with its weapon systems.

It is the same with revamping our goals.

We need to project ourselves and our vision beyond the horizon – as it's a moving horizon, expanding all the time. Even though we can't see the new goals, we must keep renewing and stretching our goals further. Setting our targets beyond the horizon. Renewing our goals and Counting new Chickens is a sure-fire way to stretch performance beyond our 'normal' range.

Time to Download:

Remember – this is not a chance just to write down things that have been confirmed, but more importantly new things that have been learned.

If you have been reminded of something that you knew but had never done anything about, it can be classed as newly learned. 'To know and not to do, is not to know.'

Action Zone

What I have learned so far ...

What I am going to do about it/use from now on ...

13

The Ninth Principle –
Relax, Lie Back and Give Away

The planet: PLUTO
At the furthest reaches of the solar system - largest orbit.

Sometimes this principle is furthest from our minds. Sometimes it is the most difficult principle to adopt - and it requires patience to let the benefits finally arrive.

Originally these were separate principles (Lie Back, and Give Away), until I realised that what I was observing was simply two aspects or manifestations of the same principle.

Observing those people who had adopted the other principles, consciously or otherwise, it became apparent that an air of relaxation descended. This resulted from the confidence engendered by having clear focus, a clear path to follow, clear objectives, and a powerful mindset. They seemed to be viewing their achievements as an inevitable consequence, unquestioning of whether they were doing the right thing, and unquestioning about whether they were actually going to get there. And throughout history, the stories of the great achievers show the same. Successful people are often perceived as being like a swan, proceeding with deceptive pace across the water, with apparent grace and ease, whilst below the surface a powerful, urgent, focused activity takes place to generate the propulsion.

It is a case of once you have 'Set the controls for the heart of the sun' (title of an early Pink Floyd song), you let the NEXUS Principles produce the success. Once your goals are set, your chickens counted, you can afford to enjoy the journey with confidence (but not complacency), because you know with certainty that you are getting where you want to be. The journey has become an intrinsic part of the goals. The success is in living the journey on a daily basis.

Relax. You can afford to when you are following the rest of the principles. Successful people are enjoying the journey by the very definition of 'success'. If you are not enjoying the journey, you will find it impossible to class yourself as successful. So to be successful, decide to enjoy the ride.

Living for the moment. Many people only enjoy themselves in retrospect. They only enjoy happiness and success when they look back. Yes, planning is important, and persistence is important. But we also need to enjoy the journey, the process of getting there, because the journey is part of the Goals, part of the Prime Vision. We can relax because we know we are on the path we have decided upon. We can rejoice in the fact that every day is leading us on to our goals.

So relax and have confidence in the success you are creating. The success that you are acting out right now. This moment is part of the success. Success is not a point in the future. It's not about achieving something sometime in the future.

This principle is about having **Faith**. The absence of this faith will result in worry. And such worry is a waste of energy – energy which is much needed elsewhere! Without this energy, it will be more difficult to apply the other principles.

The reason most people aren't relaxed is that they aren't applying the other principles. This principle is the natural extension of the application of the other principles.

Now, don't get this relaxation confused with complacency. Be relaxed, but retain the urgency and energy and focus required to reach the targets you set along the way, in the right areas, applying the right level of intensity where it counts. When it's time to act – act. When it's not, relax.

This principle is about the ability to keep a cool head, and not panicking, whilst at the same time going all out for the finish line. You can only do this if you are not exhausted by ambient 'activity'.

It is also the ability to 'lie back into the shot'. In tennis, golf, snooker, success depends on the ability to relax into the shot. And in business, in the same way, it is crucial to allow your true abilities and talents to shine through because you are relaxing.

For those salespeople who have attended sales skills courses, or anyone who has ever been on a presentation skills course, you will know that all too often the focus is purely on skills. But all that teaches people is the things they are not doing. They know most of them. But they are now aware more acutely that they were right to be nervous about speaking publicly – after all, how could they possibly remember to do all those technical things, and remember all those tricks and techniques.

No – although skills are important, relaxing into the shot is often the best way of getting the most out of your performance.

It is about being Powerful and Effortless.

Not Effort-ful and Powerless !

Start by Being Selfish!

But the first step in being relaxed is to start by being Selfish!

Yes, Selfish! In other words, in order to give of your best where it is most needed and where you can add the greatest value, you first need to be definite about what YOU want. You need to be selfish about what you want first, then have the space to be abundant for others.

Because you become grounded on your own path which is the life you love to lead, you can then offer far more of yourself to the rest of the world.

Remember, you can't walk other people's journeys for them. Nor can you walk every path that opens up in front of you and appears to be 'worthwhile'. You must be self-oriented so much that when you decide to tread a path you can do so with unequivocal energy and focus and commitment, to the benefit of others also.

I have seen far too many people derailed because they tried to be all things to all people and the only person to suffer was themselves.

Counting Chickens is about setting clear Visions for your life and having goals in the key areas which make up that life. In so doing you will have made clear decisions about what you cannot fit into your life, or do not want to fit into your life. Right now there will be activities in which you are involved, possibly overhanging from past areas of responsibility or interest, which you need to let go of. Write these down, and decide on a strategy for extricating yourself from them. Sometimes you can drop them immediately simply by not doing them anymore. Sometimes you need to carefully step away from them without destroying your relationship with others. Be firm – with yourself.

Go on, make a note right now of all those things which you need to get away from, all those extra responsibilities which prevent you being the best you can be in the key areas of your life.

Things I need to drop	How I am going to drop them
1	
2	
3	
4	
5	
6	
7	
8	
9	
10	
11	
12	

Spheres of influence

One of the most significant barriers to achievement of goals and leading a successful life is the constant deflection and diverse focus which is almost endemic in the hustle and bustle of the modern world. We are constantly being impacted by issues via the media, and our awareness of the wider world is so great that we can be deluded into thinking that we have some part to play in all of it – that we must devote attention to all of it. Indeed, we have all seen people arrive at work having listened to a topical item on the radio (probably whilst in a traffic queue) completely 'wound up' about the topic under discussion. Not very conducive to having a power mindset for the start of the day. Those who are successful have a habit of distinguishing where their control and input is required.

Consider the following.

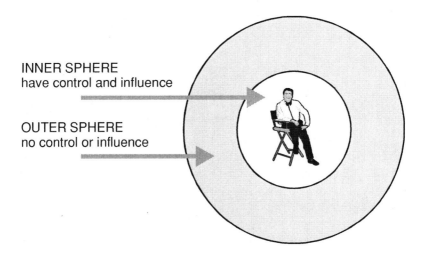

INNER SPHERE
have control and influence

OUTER SPHERE
no control or influence

When faced with an issue, decide which sphere it falls into. And if it's in the sphere of influence, then get to work on it. If it's not, then strengthen the barrier and prevent it from 'appearing' to be in your sphere of influence. This prevents frustration and impatience with issues which are not within your control.

The Serenity Prayer – by Reinhold Niebhur

**Give us the Grace to accept with serenity the things that cannot be changed,
the Courage to change the things that should be changed
and the Wisdom to distinguish one from the other.**

2am Solutions

Waking up at an unearthly hour in the night and not being able to get back to sleep because of a work-related issue which you are unsure how to handle is seen as an occupational hazard by many. In fact, it is during the resting hours that many people get their best ideas. So combining these two factors led to this stratagram.

Write down specifically the issue you wish to tackle. Then write down two options at each end of the spectrum – option 1 and option 2. Then look for a third option. This is not necessarily a 'middle option' or a compromise. It is not a 'fudge'. When you write your first two options down, they set the mind racing. They will also be a reflection of your state of mind, based on deep-seated first impressions, or paradigms about the issue and people involved. The third option will have exorcised all of these and will allow you to put together a solution with which you are confident.

This will allow you to rest, and return to sleep. And that is the object of the stratagram. The objective is to allow you to work through an issue and then rest. Well rested, you may find the next day that you do apply the third option. Or you might find that your subconscious has found a better way in the night, and as you arrive at your place of work in the morning, you come up with a better option. The key is to have a means of working through your thoughts on paper when too troubled to sleep, enabling you to put the issue to rest and for you to get rest yourself.

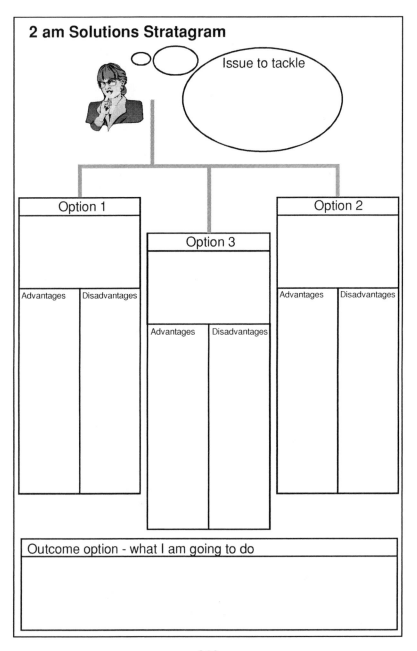

The law of increasing returns

The ability to give away comes from a sense of abundance which comes from our personal faith in our success, our journey. It derives from our powerful mindset. If there is such abundance that we can afford to give so much, then we are exercising faith in so much more arriving to replenish!

Successful people utilise fully the law of increasing returns. If you give unequivocally, you will receive back much, much more. And, often the rewards come from unimagined sources. This is the 'boomerang factor'.

I know of at least one business person who attributes much of his success to the writing of at least one 'Thank you' letter every day. This is his personal rule, a performance standard. And it gets noticed.

I read recently of a report claiming that the whole population of the world is linked through only six levels of acquaintance. This is the real World Wide Web. So saying 'thank you' in writing at least once per day is like putting a banner headline as to your good character onto this Network. Wonderful marketing, as long as it is heartfelt. And remember the return is a by-product. So don't take the action in order to get a specific reaction. That will be seen as manipulative. If this is done genuinely, simply have faith that it is the right thing to do.

Do not Give in order to Earn. But Give – and you will earn.

Coincidences are the manifestation of the law of increasing returns in action. These opportunities are sent to support, but so many people dismiss them, laughing, and just say, 'What a coincidence.' They don't act on the 'coincidence', Of course, such events were created by us, in some way, somewhere, at some time in the past. So accept the returning gift. And use it.

The Boomerang Factor

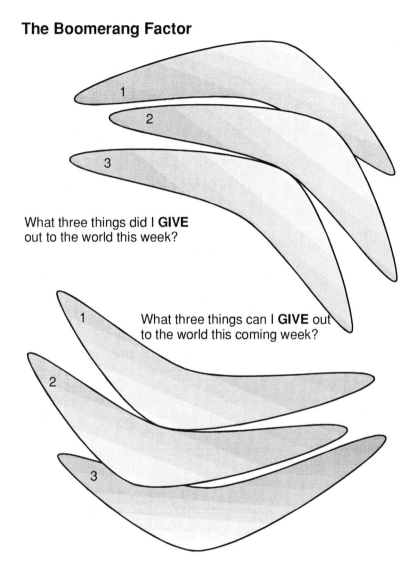

What three things did I **GIVE**
out to the world this week?

What three things can I **GIVE** out
to the world this coming week?

The Work/ Life balance misnomer

If you have been following the rest of this book up till now, I am sure
you will be able to write this section and understand it's essence from

211

the title. It amazes me how so many people discuss this topic as if work and life were two separate and diametrically opposed features. Work is one of the factors which make up life. Just as personal, social, family and so on. It may be one of your six key areas.

If you have set your Prime Vision and your plan as we covered in Section one, you will have created a balance in all areas of your life. For those who are unsuccessful, the challenge (and their perception of Work versus Life) is a direct consequence of not setting goals in this congruent way. Work is not a detractor from life. It is the tool which helps to achieve the other factors of life. It is the enabling facet of our existence. The difficulty for so many is that they see it as:

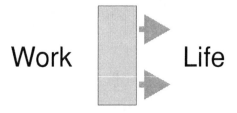

Work   Life

On the work side, they see urgency, specific objectives (set by others). And on the Life side, there is a void. No goals. No sense of direction. The line gets pushed towards the vacuum, and before long the Work has taken over.

Better to view it as six areas all interconnected.

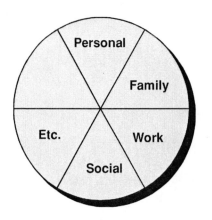

Having Goals, targets, tasks, and productivity in each area will ensure a balance is maintained and a Full life is lived.

Recharging your Battery 6-Pack

This Stratagram is all about maintaining balance by recharging your batteries in those parts of your life which need it most.

Taking the six key areas of your life, label each battery accordingly in the box underneath. Then write a score out of 10 for your current level of delight (not just satisfaction!) in that area. Go with your 'gut-feeling' here as this will tell you most about how you really feel, deep down.

Next, draw a mark on the battery cylinder representing the score you have assigned to that area of your life. So, if you have given your Health and Fitness battery a score of three, put a line about one third of the way up the battery. Once you have marked each battery, shade the lower half. You will be left with a very clear visual indication of where you need to recharge your life and where you need to focus to get back on track.

This whole stratagram is about identifying potential balance challenges early so that you can quickly address them.

It is a very valuable feature of every Hotel Day agenda!

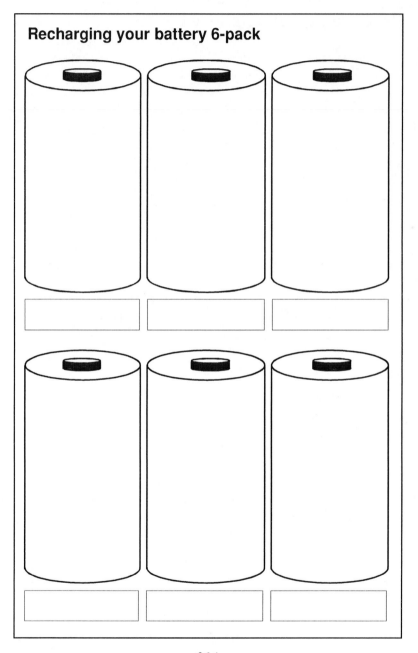

Recharging your battery 6-pack

Time to Download:

Remember – this is not a chance just to write down things that have been confirmed, but more importantly new things that have been learned.

If you have been reminded of something that you knew but had never done anything about, it can be classed as newly learned. 'To know and not to do, is not to know.'

Action Zone

What I have learned so far ...

What I am going to do about it/use from now on ...

14

First Steps – Giant Steps

So there you have it. Nine principles to help you make those chickens hatch. But, of course, it doesn't end there. Now it's your chance to apply them. And, as always, the first steps are most important. Set aside time to review and put into action all those good intentions which have appeared in your Action Zones throughout.

Many people start a new year, or reach a point of transition, feeling that a change of job or career or business will on its own create the changes to solve all their problems and create immediate success. But the changes needed in order to reach true success are not just changes in environment or job or circumstances. I hope that throughout I have been able to show that it is more about developing habits of excellence which enable you to perform at a peak, and in having the right mindset and approach to whatever you do, whatever your role, whatever your goal. It is about building world-class habits from within.

The most joyous and solemn commitment many take on in life is with the words 'I do.' That commitment is not passive – it's active commitment – I DO.

I hope that you will now do the things you want to do, to make the changes you want to make and reach the life you want to lead.

Whether your goal is immediately apparent, and has been from the moment you opened this book, or it's something you are hoping to find with the help of this book; and whether it's setting up a new business, taking an existing business to new levels, recommitting to a current career, or approaching your whole life in a new way, I hope you will find the inspiration you need.

Wishing you every success.

Afterword

"Don't Count your Chickens before they hatch!"

One of my mother's favourites. Many parents say it. We all say it. But my mother said it particularly often to me. It became a standing joke.

At the start, I suggested two incidents to shape my own thinking here. The first I outlined in chapter one. And I promised I would tell the second briefly.

It happened earlier, but the significance only surfaced later for me. In fact the significance grows the more I think about it.

27th October 1995. Bad news. I rush 350 miles to a hospital bedside. But too late. My mother has passed away, just a few minutes before I arrive. My sister, Catherine, tells me my mother's final message:

'Tell Philip – don't worry.'

I am sure I don't have to explain the significance.

Phil Olley

Keynote Business Speaker

Performance Coach

'Creating success from the inside'

For information or details about the services provided, contact:

Phil Olley Consulting

Phoenix House

Houston Avenue

Pitcairn

Glenrothes

Fife, KY7 6FL

Tel: +44 (0) 1592 563393

Fax: +44 (0) 1592 563394

Web: www.PhilOlleyConsulting.co.uk